SOLU~

FOR

DYSFUNCTIONAL

FAMILY RELATIONSHIPS:

HEALING & AVOIDING

THE

AFTERMATH

OF

CROSS-CULTURAL UNIONS

HRU YUYA.T. ASSAAN-ANU

ANU NATION
BEHIND ENEMY LINES

SOLUTIONS FOR DYSFUNCTIONAL FAMILY RELATIONSHIPS
HRU Yuya T. Assaan-Anu
Anu Nation
www.AnuNation.org

HRU Yuya T. Assaan-ANU

"SOLUTIONS FOR DYSFUNCTIONAL FAMILY RELATIONSHIPS"
© 2012, HRU Yuya T. Assaan-ANU
Anu Nation
www.AnuNation.org

This work is dedicated to the children of cross-cultural unions. I will that you find true unity and peace in your life and families.

To my parents, you have given me the gift of a diverse childhood. Your efforts to tap into my silent genius have not gone wasted. The tree that you fed and nurtured will provide you shade in your golden years.

To my daughter, Asaata Imani Assaan-ANU, I place another work at your feet. Baby Girl, you are an inextinguishable flame of brilliance, strength, and happiness. For all the praise that I receive; know that it is OUR praise that we share together. I am proud of you. You are the perfecting princess who will one day claim your place on your throne as a sovereign Empress. All that I do is for your ascension. Rise and Shine Baby Girl!

To the wombmyn who empower me through their undying devotion to the ANU family, you are my heart and soul. It is your warmth and honor that assures me of the potential of my own inspiration.
We are the Village!
Ngiyakuthanda!

To my brothers, it is OUR season to show the true power of spirit and timeless wisdom.

To Baba Gil Scott Heron, our time shared left me with many gems. You helped me to better appreciate my relationship with my own child. Thank you for the constant guidance, interest in my own art, sweet potato pies, backstage invites, and basketball games. I thank you for inviting me into your life and embracing me as family. Soar through the star systems as high as you please and may you never be the angel who falls to the dust. ASE, ASE, ASE O!!!

I offer gratitude to all of the beneficent forces who guide and harmonize my life with the divine tone. To my Egun, I offer this literary libation. You are always present and never forgotten. May you be ascended into the highest heavens every time this is read.

Let's all mend the fracture pieces
and build OUR overdue NATION!

HRU Yuya T. Assaan-ANU

<u>CONTENTS</u>

YOU DIVIDED
SO, THEY CONQUERED

HRU Yuya T. Assaan-ANU

Cultural Division amongst those engaged in long-term relationships (dating, matrimonial, sibling, parent, children, or extended family) has opened the door to an organism that has proven to be one of the most diabolical self regenerative forms of internal sabotage causing the finest of people to completely lose their will to advance, sanely, through life. For the purposes of this book we'll refer to this false happiness or, often known disaster, as "Cross-Cultural Unions". Ironically, there is no unity in this sort of arrangement and herein lies the issue. The delusional idea of cultural amalgamation within what should be a mono-organism is a false happiness overshadowed by catastrophe. This internal division feeds and nurtures external predators looking to do nothing but, conquer, steal, kill, and destroy.

"Family" can be defined as the fundamental group of any so-ciety which consists of two or more individuals with the same goals and objectives. Originally family was defined by those who served the household. This is an old definition with new world relevancy. If the family or home is an entity unto itself, the members who reside under this entity should show supreme allegiance to it. As they serve it, it serves them. How this family is served is defined by home culture.

Culture defines how race, sex, religion, education, morality, psychology, and the world as a whole are perceived. Culture is a living breathing organism that fights for survival and dominance within the psyche of an individual and community. Therefore, two cultures will fight for dominance if placed in the same space. If these cultures are forced to exist together in a unit, that unit will turn on itself and much like an organic body whose immune system begins to war with itself. Yes, Cross Cultural blending within a familial structure is a suicidal/genocidal virus and should be treated as such. It lends to disharmony, internally and externally. This virus thrives in environments such as those where individuals gain higher knowledge after engaging in a relationship with one who chooses to "fly close to the ground". The scenario expresses itself despite new religious/spiritual awakenings, and the adaptation of newly discovered universal truths.

Cross Cultural relationship/family blending has created a social aftermath resembling the butchery of militaristic miscegenation designed to bewilder a once unified people. As a result of desperation, the lack of Elderly guidance, and impractical ambitions this social virus of megalithic proportion has been running rampant throughout the homes of many oblivious people. It's torn a hole through families and birthed several generations of culturally stunted progeny. The monstrous behemoth of split camp families and torn cultural loyalties is all too often capitulated by the forced and even overconfident joining of two culturally adverse paradigms.

This work deals with the thorny course that lies before individuals and couples who find themselves in merger with people who are of a cultural standing that opposes the longevity of their own. This book will highlight this challenge that many of us are currently faced with and, more significantly, will outline the various solutions to rectifying this most heinous condition.

THE GENES OF ISIS

Nile and Kenya
Purpose

The drums were electric. The smells were alluring. The view of the beautiful brown people with broad noses, wide hips, expansive shoulders, and perfected ellipses of napped hair was glorious. Nile stood at the entrance hall of the conference center where the workshops were being held. This was the annual Kwanzaa fest and he signed up for 3 different workshops. Nile could hardly contain his excitement at the thought of what he was about to learn. He was on his way to the Afrakan Language clinic and reveled in the thought of being able to finally speak a language of his very own that would not be understood by everyone in his company.

Nile stood 6'2 and a solid 235lbs. His braided hair hung down in cornrows beyond his neck line countering his strong brow and intense hawk like eyes. Walking through the door, looking more like an athlete more than the holistic doctor that he was, he made his rounds throughout the space; stopping at each vendor stand and examining the various cultural wares. There was about fifteen minutes before the language workshop began and he figured he'd eat up some time by looking for some dub music and natural hair care products. Along the way he exchanged niceties with the multitude of people he had recognized and who knew him through the various community works he committed himself to. Nile was a well respected holistic healer with a gift for speedily distinguishing ailments that exclusively affected certain ethnic communities.

Finally, it was 11:55; five minutes until the language workshop. Nile strode over to the room where the workshop was being held and removed his notepad and pen from his bag on the way. There were already a few students engaged in multi-lingual conversation. Nile recognized a few of the faces as he walked to the front of the room penning his name to the sign-in sheet. No sooner than he finished signing his name he looked up and saw what appeared to be the instructor of the workshop making her way to the front of the class salutations of the students already in attendance.

Kenya.

She was a wombmyn hard to ignore; possessing the presence of someone far beyond her years. Kenya was graceful but, her movements seemed to come from an inner calmness rather than the finishing or etiquette instruction given to her by a maternal figure. She was the innocence of untouched sensuality. Kenya had a way about her that purely hypnotized those in her presence. She was a natural educator who could make any subject matter engaging, clear, and down-to-earth with a magnetism that impassioned her listeners. One could get high off of her presence.

Kenya, a multi-linguist and prolific writer, was licensed to teach the class this year. After settling the participants and delivering a succinct, but provocative, bio about herself Kenya went on to instruct the captive participants on the importance of reclaiming language and then went on to teach, for three hours, various phrases and terms in Bantu.

Nile was impressed.

At the conclusion of the class he hastily gathered his learning supplies and rushed to the bathroom in order to refresh himself for the next workshop he pre-registered for entitled, "Establishing and Operating Community Based Organizations". By the time Nile waited in line to use the bathroom sink he was about five minutes late for the workshop and ended up having to sit in the rear of the large lecture hall. His view was terrible but, at least he was able to make out the slide projections and hear the presenter clearly. Nile enjoyed another flawless clinic. At its finale he decided he'd take the opportunity to catch up with the class facilitator, whom he'd known for some time; Baba Freeman. He was a respected Elder and educator who had a far-reaching demonstrative community building track record. Nile wished to share some of his own plans with him and possibly initiate a Jegna/apprentice rapport with him. Nile had many discussions with Baba Freeman and had even been enlisted by him and his wife, Iya Freeman, as their family doctor on several occasions. As Nile approached him he noticed Baba Freeman already walking towards him with his arms outstretched flashing his distinctive smile that he'd make with one eye closed. Baba Freeman was a well built but, compact man with radiant skin and a dazzling mane of thick locs that swung down below his kneecaps.

Baba Freeman was a small man but, even at the age of seventy-four had no gut, only speckles of gray in his full head of hair, and had bright eyes that darted back and forth with alertness.

Baba Freeman called out to Nile and walking briskly to him gave him a strong embrace, which the large man was gladdened by. Slightly lifting Nile off his feet, Nile thought that the years of working with Baba Freeman had paid off and this man who was well into his seventies had the strength of a man one-third his age. Nile was a good physician and, more significantly, a caring warrior healer who took a personal interest in each of the clients he worked with.

After exchanging good-natured remarks with the young man, the elder informed Nile that he had someone he wanted to introduce him to. Nile walked to the front of the room with Baba Freeman and returned to his lecture podium; sitting there was Kenya.

Sheba and Thomas
Virtual Reality

"Submit"

She stood there looking at her laptop screen in disbelief. She could hardly believe that she'd been reduced to posting an online personal in order to find the man that would serve as the father of her future children and life compliment.

She felt stings of shame.

It's not as though she hadn't explored all of the options that she respectfully could but, sadly, she had her fill of wasteful dating excursions and failed relationships.

Sheba was a simple wombmyn; one that could be considered attractive but, not necessarily pretty by societal standards. She had a close cropped natural hairstyle that drew attention to her features which, if she had more hair would probably be considered indistinguishable. She donned the skin tone of bronzed amber and pronounced facial features that could be seen from a distance adjoining a gap toothed smile with slight dental over bite.

"So, that's it."

She felt as though she entered a new era but, at the same time, sunk to an all time low. The feeling that rose up through the soles of her feet was one of uneasiness and embarrassment. She reflected on her recent discoveries and self improvements spurned by her coming into, what she considered a higher awareness and deeper acquaintance with herself. She'd gone from Rites of Passage, initiating into a traditional Indigenous religion, cutting her perm out and sporting a natural, she even legally changed her name; all to pay tribute to the newly rediscovered truths she had learned about herself and her ethnic origins. She was proud of her work and the improvement she'd seen in many areas of her life but, having to post an on-line ad....made her feel as though she'd been punished for wanting to invest in and live her own culture. It was confusing.

Sure, she'd attempted to meet men at events she attended and even gave some guys her number whom she'd met at "Liberation Bookstore", the local juice bar/book store. It seemed as though the more "deep" they were, the more infantile their behavior. She felt she didn't want much...only authenticity and someone who was living what they preached. She had dated guys with names starting with vowels and full of hyphens that spanned the entire width of a piece of paper. They'd walk around with a drum or a saddlebag full of books, incense, and fruit... the type who'd address every wombmyn as empress, queen, or goddess. She'd been so excited the first time she dated one of these grassroots, front line, down for the cause "brothas". What a disappointment. She found herself still dealing with the same dysfunction, in men, she thought she'd left (no job or desire to generate revenue, transient lifestyle, no life plan, children scattered over several states with no working relationship with their mother's, unreliable, tardy, uncouth, etcetera, etcetera). What a letdown. Initially, she just knew every brother with locs, a cool demeanor, and who traded their b-boy stance for a militant's posture would be her very own Huey P. Newton or Kwame Nkrumah. Some of these "brothas" even had the impudence to approach her about polygyny but, could hardly take care of themselves, let alone tend to two wives. She had even tried dating some men from her church but, as she learned and saw more, she realized she had less and less in common with believers and felt a deeper kinship with "knowers".

As she decided to make herself an apple and ginger juice with the new high powered blender, she loved using, she thought to herself about the feelings of lonesomeness that she'd been struck with ever since she embarked on this journey to discover her forgotten past. Sheba had made the mistake of romanticizing what she envisioned as being a whirlwind affair of learning and renewal. In fact she now had more questions than answers and found herself occasionally depressed by what she was now able to see so clearly, although the circumstances of her and her people had been right in front of her throughout her entire lifetime. It appeared as though there was more of a support structure put in place for people who were living the life of ignorant blissfulness. It seemed unfair. Sheba also had desires to have a child and just saw no hope in sight unless she surrendered her morals.

Just as the blender completed its whirling motion and Sheba headed to the other side of the kitchen to begin cleaning out the blender she heard an incoming message chime in on her laptop. She thought to herself as she took a large gulp of her ginger tonic, as if it were a strong shot of bourbon, "could someone have replied that soon?" "No, girl, you're acting a little too desperate right about now". As she sauntered over to the laptop she thought about how silly she'd feel if the email that just arrived was a piece of Spam mail telling her she had $100k waiting for her in a foreign bank account or an invitation to try a sexual libido drug. She laughed within and prided herself on her new found ability to laugh at herself taking life lightly.

SUBJECT: In response to your on-line ad looking for a true life partner.

OK, let the games begin.

Spencer and Tracey
The Pedestal

Spencer loved to watch Tracey in action. She was a powerful presence and a formidable challenger to any life obstacle. "Pull!" she yelled out and the disc went flying in the air to only be shattered moments later by Tracey's rifle blast. She was an impeccable shot and if not for her small stature she would have made skeet shooting appear to be an utterly effortless activity. Though they had begun the activity together, Spencer was not the prodigy Tracy was. Spencer had already begun breaking down his firearm and was ready to head inside and get a bite to eat before the long drive back into the city. Once Tracey had her fill of releasing the thunderous boom of her fire stick, the two began to make their way over to the dining pavilion.

Spencer and Tracey had known one another all their lives. They had both ran track together and were even student members of the "Business Leaders of Tomorrow" club. Their families had known each other intimately and their parents shared a long history. It was always known that Spencer and Tracey would end up together one day as they seemed as close as brother and sister even more than their own biological brothers and sisters.

In high school Spencer was well known as a star athlete and student body president. He had the handsome looks of an R&B crooner and an incredibly pleasant way about him that could disarm anyone who had the delight of making his acquaintance. Spencer stood an even six feet tall and through the years was able to maintain his runners physique with his broad shoulders, V shaped back, and chiseled features. He averted the rounded out facial features and form of most of his age group.

Tracey had always been Spencer's devoted backbone and confidant. In their younger years it was her idea for him to run for student body president and she was the greatest campaign manager that anyone could ever desire. Tracey was a woman of mammoth drive and talent. She graduated at the top of her class, served as the class valedictorian at her college graduation, and was a well known and respected program director for an international organization dedicated to advocating the rights of refugee women from abusive cultures. Yes, Tracey was the epitome of the take charge woman. Her father had even nick-named her "Major" and through the years the family moniker affirmed its accuracy via her demonstration.

Tracey stood at 5'4 with a physique that was well developed. On the track team her specialty had been the shot-put and with her extraordinarily muscular lower body and chiseled abdomen it was no wonder how she had set records, still unbroken, throughout her high school and college tenure. Tracey, "Major", was a woman who preferred plain uncomplicated attire and rarely was seen with a hairstyle other than a ponytail. She kept her makeup to a minimum as she had such beautiful skin and bright eyes, it would only mask the radiance of her optimum health. Though she was a woman of relatively small stature most people thought her much taller and larger than she actually was. Tracey had presence and knew how to call people to attention and reduce them with the intimidating glare that she perfected over the years.

Spencer loved the way Tracey could always snap him back to reality and get him on course. He was attracted to the unwavering flame that she always seemed to carry. He, himself, hadn't been nearly as consistent as she'd been. Although he never had much difficulty in obtaining the things he wanted in life, he inwardly could confess that he wanted very little. He had worked as a technical recruiter ever since his senior year in college and enjoyed his work well enough. He got to fly around the country recruiting new talent for the engineering firm he worked for, had access to a hefty expense account, company car, and quarterly bonuses depending on his performance. Even with that his greatest pride was Tracey. He loved the way she knew what to do in every situation and seemed to always plan so far in advance that she was never caught off guard.

They were what one would consider a power couple and despite Tracey's aggressiveness and Spencer's complacency, they had a calm enough relationship. The fact that their families were so close made things a bit awkward at times as there always seemed to be new expectations and pressures put on the two but Spencer and "Major" did alright for themselves, all the same.

HRU Yuya T. Assaan-ANU

CULTURE

Control what you think about yourself and you will control what you

do about yourself

From the Latin "colere" meaning to "cultivate".

Culture is the all encompassing self regenerating organism that defines a society's way of operating in the physical and spiritual world. Culture or the developmental element defines spirituality of a society, logic, tradition, societal norms, perspective, objectives, economics, politics, education, art, values, language, and disposition of a people. Culture also holds its own built-in defense mechanisms.

Cultural indoctrination is the anticipated end result of religious, educational, political, institutions and organizations of sports and entertainment. Through these various channels one can begin to contour the functional, or dysfunctional, mind of a people for various purposes. In the case of children, through the use of mythology, fairy tales, collective norms of disciplining, and **media,** the developing mind of a child is shaped and formed. There are indelible impressions that stain the cerebral of us all in our youth that, if needed to, can take an entire lifetime to remove from the imprinted mind. The impact of what we ingest and accept as fact or truth is typically the reference we use to pilot our lives for our entire life cycle. Without fully innerstanding the origins of our own cultural mind we fly on auto-pilot with hopes of reaching our life's destination.

Note: If you do not assert a culture for yourself one will be chosen for you.

There are some who function under the delusion that culture is a supplementary life choice or cursory activity. This is a dangerous posture as it immediately reveals one who is operating under the hand of a culture that they've been unknowingly indoctrinated with.

Music, wardrobe, and language are all products and, concurrently, sustainer of culture but they are not the culture themselves. They are cultural identifiers. So, one sharing a certain type of music or wearing a certain type of garb is not necessarily spreading culture but, can more precisely be defined as showing evidence of their own cultural investment. Culture is not something that can be swapped flippantly like a pair of shoes or hairstyle. Culture is a complex multi-layered mechanism that, much like the human ego, fights for its survival. It's an organic symbiotic organism that entwines itself into the mind of all of its constituents. In order to properly identify the most opportune cultural posture one must have knowledge of self.

It is possible to have a cultural root that is a permutation of diverse cultural influences that subsequently birth a new singular culture. This is healthy and culturally responsible. Now is a time when problem solvers are needed possessing the bravery to re-engineer culture and community norms to work in their best interest. Culture will always fight to maintain its presence as it is a living, evolving spirit. The transfigurations that culture twists and forms into should be an indication of the progression of a society and not the devolving of a collective consciousness.

The reclamation of lost culture and defining of a common way lies at the core of any evolutionary or spirit centering struggle. Common culture is the unifying field.

Culture in opposition

Two cultures cannot coexist within the same home. Over time one culture will naturally strive to ascend to the dominant position. This brings one culture to the recessive and the other to the dominant. In this instance what will happen is the culture that was forced to take the recessive position will begin to resent the culture in the dominant position. This, unavoidably, lends itself to domestic tension and opposition. When individuals join as a couple or family unit what should be created is one culture birthed from the adjoining cultural influences. This new home culture doesn't, necessarily, need to confirm or mirror any extraneous cultural model but, most significantly, must work for the advancement of the unit. Adaptive re-engineering of the familial unit is necessary and recommended for the joining of separate cultural postures. What we're speaking about here is the culture that exists between healthy couples based on the awareness of gender based roles and responsibilities.

This may seem antithetical to the new-age notion of universality; but, in truth, communities/families that have demonstrated vitality and who thrive develop a single cultural imperative despite any extraneous influences.

MATE SELECTION

Here lays the "Genesis" of potential issues so, let us examine some common scenarios and the potential fixes for them as this is where the softness or bumpiness of the forthcoming road is determined. Mate selection can either be done with keen foresight, as a preventive measure, or it can be done recklessly with the *hopes that things will work themselves out on their own; but, this is the fundamental juxtaposition of one of the most important choices in this entire process.

*Hope is a product of anxiety.

Life partners should be selected with shrewdness and legitimacy based research. Selecting a partner based on bio-electric stimuli (reactive feelings), ROMANtic fantasy, presumed societal expectations, misguided religious obligations, or any other short-sighted incentive will cripple, at the onset, any real chance a duo might have to actually discover and experience a valid, air-tight union. When filtering out prospective familial partners it is important not to blunt your own awareness of right and exactness with the distorted cautions of societal gender stereotypes. Truth blurs with unverifiable excess introspection. Truth must be activated through action. The thought of concession of principle or essential requisites must not enter into the picture but, one must be clear on what is needed to insure sustainability of their home and comeunity. This should be the primal source of enthusiasm during the process of securing a mate, not self aggrandizing fantasy.

The invasive onslaught of music, movie, and television programming has shaped the conduct and perception of the populace with regard to soliciting the love and devotion of another individual. This manufactured social reality calls for complete and undying devotion to "castle in the sky" based, unsubstantiated "rules" of intimate engagement that drive male and female alike through a never ending labyrinth of confusion and failed expectations. Failure to meet these expectations sends one into a state of depression.

There are songs which chime:
    "You are my all in all"
    "Without you, I'm nothing"
    "I'd die for you"
    "You are my everything"
    And so on and so on....

These terms make love and intimate affairs a mortal act of fanatical religious salvation. Your relationship should be a religion but, a religion that evolves you to your altitudinous place, not into further servitude with a devotion to ideas and customs that you can't identify with nor find rationality in.

Your life partner/mate/spouse is just that. The idea that one's mate should fill the role of 10-15 people can be attributed to this lunacy. Your spouse should not fill the role of your best friend, activity partner, diviner, mother/father, or daughter/sun. This is not saying that your spouse can not function in these roles occasionally but, to put full-time demands of those roles on an individual not only begins to tear at the very fabric and understanding of community and family but, is an unrealistic burden.

What does the prospect of this union mean for your family, your community, your ethnic group? Is it likely that the union and any resulting fruit from it will be a burden to your people or will it serve to further them? There is nothing that occurs in a vacuum as an abstraction, so picking your lover poorly or under the influence of unwise counsel can set off a chain of events that could affect an entire community due to the irresponsibleness of it.

Here's a thought:

Your children are not *your* children. Your children are reincarnated Ancestors and deities who've returned to perform a cosmically commissioned task. So, carelessly selecting an individual to co-create with imposes a great trauma on your bloodline and Ancestors; similar to inviting a beloved community Elder over for the evening and setting a plate of elbow scabs and foot calluses in front of them to eat; and if that weren't enough taking them to a bedroom to rest on a bed of bloody ice picks.

Is this the welcome that OUR Ancestors deserve? Consider, wisely the channels you present to them for their arrival and care taking.

I've seen many cases where Wombmyn will select anyone to co-create with because inwardly they feel the child is more theirs, as mother. This is an asinine thought. Spiritually and biologically both bloodlines can lay claim to the progeny of such a union and the child can choose to manifest the disposition or aspirations of either parent, no matter how much one believes they can train the other parent out of them. Beyond the genetic aesthetic value look to the potential partners ability to tune into the unseen world, intelligence, spiritual authority, physical health, possible lineage markers, and so on. You would not attempt to mate a thoroughbred horse with a jack-ass...or would you? Likewise, in ancient times bloodlines were not mixed randomly on a whim. Now, consider if who you're mating with even comes from a region or nation your Ancestors have blended well with. How do you know you're not reuniting two historical warring nations? What will exist inside of your home?

War.

The phenomenal nature of a well balanced relationship is superseded by, solely, the productions and offspring of that relationship. This balance begins with the individual knowing their natural divine role in the context of the universe. There can be no identity crisis on the part of either Man or Wombmyn. The presence of an identity crisis leads to gender confusion and the aspiring of synthetic roles based on an artificial intelligence. One must exhaustively research, and more significantly, live out and put to practice the highest ideas of their own gender designation. The role of Man or Wombmyn in a relationship cannot be merely theorized.

Mate selection is a science. It need not be a safari of trial and error. Through too much trial and error the egoistic mind will do nothing but, work to affirm the dysfunctional notions handed down through societal stereotypes. One should lay down a documented set of standards...a list of qualities and characteristics they see as central in their envisioned mate. This will serve as a reference point when encountering prospects so that energy and emotions are not expended pointlessly.

Idyllically one should look for a well-matched partner while doing the work of their life purpose. In doing this you attract other's to you engaged in the same activities and most likely who have similar convictions as your own.

<u>DATING</u>
Where things begin is where they will end.

During this time "illusion preservation" can bring the most monstrous of consequences. Ignoring the "red flags" of forthcoming cross-cultural carnage help no one but, only serve to delay the inescapable. The various dating scenarios are open to subjective judgment and discernment but, ultimately dating/ courting should be purposeful. Burning time and energy investing in outings that are solely entertainment based rarely provide individuals opportunity to actually learn one another; sometimes this is done intentionally. There are people who will keep themselves in disguise for as long as they can maintain the masquerade knowing full well that their character, at its core, is defected.

For the purposes of this work we will use the term "courting" or "court" to allude to the process of two individuals undergoing a process of discovering mutual interest and character for the purposes of establishing a long term relationship. This allusion is not altogether accurate with the etymological root of the word. "Courting" or "Court" is an expression that was originally defined as a "yard" or "enclosed space". So to court someone, in the old sense of the word, would be described as an act of wooing and paying homage to an individual in order to lure them into an enclosed space. Similarly to what happens in a court of law. An attorney woos an unsuspecting defendant into enclosed space (jail) through deception and wooing. This definition still motivates far too many of the "courting" processes that exist today.

As a meeting location there are few places that succeed natural environments for building a rapport with another. There are no hard-set rules when it comes to actual activities or the chaperoned versus unchaperoned format however, it is advisable to balance isolated outings with those that are done within the context of community. Spending time observing how one is received by the greater comeunity and the fluidity of their social skills allows for enhanced character circumspection. Dating can even be goal centered. It may be unusual, but not unrealistic, to set benchmarks throughout the dating process for what information or concepts to cover during the shared time.
For example:

Date 1 - Discuss one another's cultural perspective and world view.

Date 2 - Attend a cultural comeunity event and discuss its relevance.

Date 3 - Exchange long term plans

Date 4 - Confer with another couple of Elder status

This is a very loose outline that offers purpose and definition to the dating experience.

Utilize partner litmus test to filter out those bringing nothing to the table other than a *fork* and *plate*. If you have responsibly designed a plan for your life journey, it is fair to expect someone who desires to blend with your life to have made an equal investment. A purpose driven dating design will instantly reveal any bona fide or artificial declarations that exist in word only.

Outings should reflect the life path and culture that each partner is looking to head in. In other words, one should not judge mates viability by their ability to meet the standards of an alien culture. Because you're taken to an expensive french restaurant or an italian opera you should not be lead to believe that one is cultured, creative, or even socially capable unless those outings reflect the cultural origins of that person. So, sisters, if he proposes to take you to an Afrakan dance troupe performance and then get a bite to eat at a Black owned juice bar, do not consider him lowly. He is expressing his own cultural investment and pride to you. Do not judge him by someone else's standards that, in truth, apply to neither one of you.

Be true to what you are in all moments and occasions. Do not rob anyone of their precious rationing of time by not being forth coming about your intention and true character from the commencement of a budding relationship. If you don't desire to be known do not require anyone to make themselves known to you. Confirm equality and reciprocity at all times. If you are in a place in your life where you are still attempting to find out who/what/where you are, allow that process to march on without external misdirection or perversion. What could be more important that knowing you? Once you have grasped the authenticity of your own inner truth, you can use that truth as a standard to gauge others by. Judge the spirit of truth with the spirit of truth.

Do not engage in missionary dating. That is to say, do not try to convert those you date from their own cultural perspective

10

to your own. In this you become no different than a colonizer. If you're constantly at odds in terms of cultural perspective, with your object of adoration then it would be wise to lay both of your quintessential cultural imperatives on the table and judge them for congruency by universal laws. This, too, can be an exercise in futility if there is no joint agreement on what is to be considered ancient and universal between you two and if that is the case; your relationship is destined to decline. There can, and should, be unique expressions of core values but, ultimately those core values must be the synoptic. The family plan and value system should be discussed and agreed upon prior to the actual creation of family. If you initiate your relationship from a place of division, it will be just that easier for external forces to widen the divide and "pick-off" the fragmented family members.

There is only the feminine principle

As wombmyn, you should be in position to cultivate and expand on whatever you are given by your mate. Be the fertile soil your family needs. You are the primordial and postpartum indoctrinator of family culture. Your ability to listen and be the active force is key. As you will, undoubtedly, surpass your ideal mate in emotional intelligence, open your heart to someone who dwarfs you in logical intellect. This is not a competition. He must have a plan, demonstrated ability to lead, and a broader perspective than that of your own in order to properly cover you and your children. Accept no boyish behavior. What is he building? Tell him "NO HAMMERS, NO HUGS". Look for one who can lead you and bring order to your thoughts and feelings that you have which may still be formless. This is his job. He should be your counterbalance of rationale and physicality. Do not test his resolve trough antagonism and debate. He will eventually see you as less than feminine because of this and will reason if you're more male than female, you certainly don't need his presence/ support and he'll eventually want nothing to do with you or what you two produce. Maintain your femininity at all times. This is the only way he can securely and truthfully interlock with you.

Man, what is your plan?

Are you prepared to look into the eyes of your loved one/ ones as they await your direction and plot the next move with confidence and surefooted knowing? If not, you must train as an Asafo (warrior scholar) until you can show the proven ability to do so. Your wombmyn is your spiritual and emotional sentinel. She has sensitivity in these respective concentrations which you may never comprehend. You must look for her to compliment you in this way; never discredit the worth of a sensitive wombmyn by toying with her emotional sensitivities. In the same manner never allow yourself to be emotionally bullied by her or anyone else. You may be the strength of the come-unity but, she is the power center of that same come-unity. Her allegiance should be to her spiritual convictions and then to your family plan; and there should be no discrepancies.

Be clear, as well, how you met her sets the standard for what she supposes you will accept. If her attire was revealing and vulgar when you met do not demand that she alters one thread for your personal benefit. This is selfish and these types of control dramas will only breed turmoil and confusion. One can educate their partner on proper attire but, unless there is a desire to evolve, jointly, you are wasting your time and energy. Take time to explain and educate, never try to convince or sway. Powerful wombmyn do not mistake sexuality for sensuality or coyness for feminine reservation. Attach to a wombmyn who causes you to strive beyond your current station in life. If you find yourself regressing you are unequally yoked and you need to remove yourself from this role that you are currently blocking for the man who is right for this particular wombmyn. Conversely, do not fear your own refinement at the hands of a magnetic wombmyn. It is her innate natural endowment; this ability to cause those around her to rise to power. It is elating to walk with a fine wombmyn at your side but, it is a phenomenal thing to walk with a refined wombmyn at your side.

TIME SHARED

Nile and Kenya
Doing the Work

Three months had gone by. Nile and Kenya had become an indivisible pair full of creative energy and productivity. The eager couple had thrown several shared events, facilitated classes together, and had even taken several courses together. After each event, they'd always figure out a way to extend the walk to the train or take the longer way home. Nile admired Kenya to no end and Kenya had never felt so secure and happy with anyone before. They spent a good deal of time together but, interesting enough barely spoke to each other. Their interaction was full of latent communication. There was much to be said in a glance or deep breath. In the conventional sense Nile and Kenya had not had one "official" date. There had been no movie or dinner outings; only comeunity work, action meetings, and advancement courses. The extra hours, here and there, they were able to capture before and after events left them so filled afterwards that they hadn't considered that anything may had been lost in their exchanges.

Kenya began to give thought to the seriousness of this great Kingman she felt honored to spend so much time with. Nile had never flirted with her; which was something rare. She never even saw him looking at her out of the corner of his eye when she walked past him. Nile never spoke to her as though he felt a sense of ownership over her as his Queen although when they were out in public and people would refer to her as his Queen; Nile would not correct them. This pleased Kenya.

Tom and Sheba
Covert Operations

Sheba and Tom had been conversing via instant messenger, phone, and text message for a month now. They exchanged pictures of one another, video-phoned, and were both pleased with the experience. Sheba had made a conscious decision to present, as she called it, "a lighter side of Sheba" to Tom. She assumed keeping the conversations fairly surface level until they actually met in person and had an opportunity to see how they felt about one another, would be the most strategic way to proceed. Sheba witnessed, first hand, the disastrous effects of sharing too much about her cultural posture...all at once. This investiture seemed to scare men away; not to mention the clumsy, to say the least, reactions when they came to her place and saw the shrine she set up in the middle of her living room for her Ancestors. No...easing Tom in slowly would be best, she soothingly reasoned to herself. Through the course of events she'd grown weary of ruined attempts to win a mate and moved with the caution of a lioness that'd been outrun by one too many prey.

Tom was a political science professor at a local college. He'd been in education for over ten years and loved his work. He had two sons from a previous marriage. His relationship with them and their mother seemed to be amiable enough. Sheba surmised that Tom was very committed to ideas of family and stood as the backbone of his own extended family. He was a strong man. Sheba was comforted by this as it seemed men who even had the desire to create and serve a family were a lost ware. Tom was a man of great longanimity and an intense listener. He appeared like he'd not hurt a soul given the opportunity; often jovial and full of wit, exchanging with Tom was a joy. Tom would dutifully and thoughtfully text her every day just to see how she was doing. He didn't rush her to see her in person although he made it clear that he looked forward to it.

After their 4 weeks of internet and cell phone fun, they jointly agreed it was time for their first date. Tom had offered to take Sheba to see a Brazilian dance troupe and then dinner. Sheba pondered on how out of practice she felt with it all. She realized she'd not been on a real date in almost 12 months and was still waiting for her dating senses to kick in. She felt as if, lately, everything seemed to be a new excursion of wonder for her. Her time established methods of computing her steps and reactions had been reassessed and demolished by the wisdom she summoned at the foot of her alter.

Moonlight silhouetted the night. Sheba decided to wear a plain aqua blue dress and wrapped her baby locs with a brown silk scarf. She had an urge to wrap her hair up in a whirl of Afrakan fabric as she usually did but instead, she narrowed her will to express her recently discovered golden Genesis by giving an appearance of neutrality. She decided to compliment her outfit with a pair of cowrie shell earrings and matching necklace. In this she felt she left enough hint of eclecticism without giving too much information that may lead to a bitter end of the sweet affair she'd enjoyed for the past month. Her biological clock driven mission to have a family of her own was a whirling vortex poised to destroy any obstacle in its path.

Sheba was filled with congested emotion. As she waited at the park fountain that she and Tom had decided to meet at she felt bombarded by a mob of insecurities and suppressed a sensation of vertigo. She felt beautiful but, wondered if she'd be beautiful to Tom. Every breath she took seemed to overwhelm her with thoughts of possible disappointment and frustration. She felt foolish for adopting feelings that rejected her beauty... bargaining her intellect and awareness for fear of continuing through life alone. Just as her internal debate between her esteem and ego reached its apex she felt a tap on her left shoulder.

"Sheba?"

"Yes"

"It's me, Tom"

Sheba just stared.

Tom reached out his hand to greet Sheba's and when she responded in kind he pulled her closer and hugged her. Sheba, startled by this bold gesture, allowed herself to fall into his arms. She wanted to fold herself inside of his muscular arms and remain until the sunrise...secure...loved.

Tom, a man of thick proportion, stood about 5'9. He wore a thick mustache that offset his large squared jaw giving way to a huge set of teeth that lit up this husky man's entire countenance. Tom was as handsome in person as he was "digitally". He had the widest cow eyes that Sheba loved because she felt it showed evidence of above average intelligence. His clothing was loose fitting and the linen shirt and pants set he donned gave him a distinguished look. Tom reminded Sheba of a young James Earl Jones and had the booming voice to match. "Now, this, I can work with" she calculatedly thought to herself.

With arms encircling the warm body of Sheba, Tom whispered, "I'm happy you're here". Sheba replied, reflexively, "I couldn't imagine a better place to be". This was more than Sheba had prepared herself for and felt a bit silly for allowing herself to be caught up in the "rapture of Tom", but allowed herself a night of abandonment.

The dance troupe's performance was fantabulous and both Tom and Sheba were exhilarated from the music. Tom came out of the theater dancing and holding Sheba's hand in the air as if he would twirl her through the lobby. *"Yeah, I'm gonna have to teach this brother how to dance"*, Sheba thought amusingly to herself. Still it was refreshing to see a man of Tom's stature relax and enjoy his life. Tom seemed to not have a burden in the world and this attracted Sheba to him. Aside from her own work it had seemed as though much of her spare time was spent studying about the challenges and ills that faced her people. Tom allowed her to forget all that dread...if only for one night.

On their way to the restaurant Tom asked Sheba what she'd thought about the storyline of the performance. Sheba hesitated to answer. She had known the storyline was actually an Orisha tale surrounding Obatala and Osun. She didn't want to seem too in the know but, needed to gather data on Tom's reaction to traditional African religion. Sheba stated that she found it to be profound and admitted that she found African mythology to be quite interesting. Tom's reaction was difficult to read as he maintained the same boyish grin that he'd wore since exiting the theater.

At the Colombian restaurant that Tom had suggested, Sheba felt the anxiety that had plagued her earlier in the evening re-emerge. She knew that her choice of vegetarianism had caused difficulty in the past and had seemed to turn some men off. She had even compromised her eating plan in several instances and ordered fish and dairy dishes. She paid for it at the mouth of the "white porcelain god" in her bathroom and vowed never to put her digestive systems through such changes again. Now, she was confronted again with the potential clumsiness of opposing dietary preferences.

As soon as they were seated she told Tom that she would probably just order a salad because she had a hefty lunch that day. Tom feigned an immediate look of disappointment and shared with Sheba that he had in mind what he'd order for them both because, this being one of his favorite eateries, he knew the menu fairly well. "Oh well", the burly man said with a mock gesture of letdown, "I guess I should have warned you first...either way I'm just glad to break bread with you finally". Sheba was relieved. It appeared as though she wouldn't have to address the "no meat products thing" this evening.

Tom ordered healthy servings of animal carcass and even had the server pull another small table up close to theirs so he could work on his meal components concurrently. The smell of all of the cooked pork had actually sent a rush of nausea to Sheba but, she countered it with ample servings of ginger tea. Tom was a man who loved his food. She was also pleased to see a man with a healthy appetite. There was something about it that spoke to Tom's manhood.

Tom and Sheba enjoyed a night of laughter and shared childhood stories until the restaurant closed on them. They enjoyed one another's company immensely and seemed to be a good blend. Tom was completely enamored with Sheba and, although he couldn't place his finger on it, knew that there was something very different about her. Sheba owned a uniqueness of spirit and insight that Tom had not experienced before. Although she was not well versed in current events she had a remarkable grasp on the mechanics of politics and the underlying meaning of political structure and method. Actually, there was very little Tom found Sheba did not understand. At every subject she met him eye to eye. He even spoke openly about his two sons, Martin and Malcolm, and instead of the typical looks of wariness that would wring the faces of his date; Sheba perked up even more and seemed to delight in the stories he told about them. Sheba was special and Tom had no intention of letting her slip through his hands. He decided, then and there, that he'd do whatever was necessary to make and keep her happy.

DETERMINING COMPATIBILITY

Some of the points and scenarios that we've thus far covered can be used as test for compatibility. There are fundamental questions I'd advise one to ask. The following represents a sample of those questions:

- What is your life purpose?
- Are you spiritual or religious?
- At what age did you become a man or wombmyn? How did you know? Was it verified by anyone else?
- What are your top three essential requirements in a relationship? Do those requirements change if the relationship is an intimate one?
- Do you have any sexually transmitted/transmittable diseases?
- Are you holistically healthy?
- How would you define your ethnicity?
- Do you have children? Whether you do or don't, what do you feel they need in order to manifest their best? Have you put these things in place?
- What are your feelings about natural births?
- Are you most comfortable in an urban or rural setting? Why?
- How do you define economics?
- How do you define politics? What is your political posture?
- Do you have friends of your own gender?
- How would you define your world-view and life philosophy, respectively?
- Do you explore any creative expressions?
- What is your means of recharging yourself?
- What do you consider to be the roles of the man and wombmyn in a family?
- How do you feel about public education? What are your views on homeschooling?
- Would you ever consider adopting a child?
- What was your childhood like?
- Where do you see yourself in 5, 15, 25 years?
- How would you define marriage?
- How do you feel about ethnic-traditional forms of marriage?

Solutions for Dysfunctional Family Relationships

These questions represent only a sampling of areas that should be addressed before any concerted investment of time, energy, and emotion. Again, the recognition of a guiding set of universal principles is an invaluable intra-personal compass, of sorts, that can be used to reaffirm the harmony amongst family/relationship participants. The Nguzo Saba, Laws of Ma'at, Kawaida, Hermetic laws, Tao Te Ching, I-Ching, Kabbalah, and many more are excellent examples of living functional principles that can be applied and used as a set of guiding contextual reference points. This safeguard also presupposes a set of checks and balances that family members can use in order to maintain respect and balance. When authoritative family members of a family have a set of values that they are all subject to, conflicts and dilemma's can be easily resolved by comparing the merit of the issue by the tenants espoused in the set of values chosen by the family. This speaks, again, to the necessity of a common kernel culture amongst all family or relationship participants. It should go without saying that love, peace, and harmony should be the core supportive mantra for any union.

HRU Yuya T. Assaan-ANU

<u>AWAKENINGS</u>
<u>AND GROUNDINGS</u>

Sheba and Tom
Child-centric

"Run Mau Mau"
"Run! Run!"
     Sheba was yelling at the top of her lungs along with Tom and Zorah, Tom's ex-wife. Malcolm, Tom's oldest son, was running through the in-zone and about to make the 1st touchdown of the game. Malcolm, or "Mau Mau" as Sheba affectionately called him, was the star quarterback of his middle school football team. He was only 12 years old but had the same wide frame of his father; tree trunk legs and a deep barrel chest. Sheba had instantly fallen in love with Malcolm and his younger brother Martin the minute they were introduced to her. Martin, the intellectual, was as thoughtful and patient as his father. He stayed close to his mother, Zorah, and was chiefly concerned with pleasing her. He looked so much like her they were often mistaken for brother and sister, despite him being only 10 years old.

     "That's my baby", Zorah shouted from the bleachers with all of the fervor of a proud, nurturing, devoted mother. Zorah took her job of parenting very seriously and genuinely enjoyed the company of her two sons. Zorah was one of the most beautiful women Sheba had ever met and in fact many of her earlier insecurities resurfaced upon first meeting her. Zorah looked like a cross between Amel Larrieux and Angela Bassett. She had a graceful silent warrior vibe about her that seemed ancient but, also very welcoming. After she and Tom divorced she kept herself busy with her two primary objectives: 1) taking care of Malcolm and Martin and 2) Opening a drug rehabilitation center specializing in spiritual and holistic medicine. Zorah, a former attorney, was a charismatic woman who was living and walking in the conviction of her life's determination. She and Sheba had hit it off from the onset and were slowly developing a genuine sisterhood as Sheba cared for "Mau Mau and Martin" as if they'd come from her own womb.

     Three years had passed since the evening that Tom and Sheba had shared and came to know as their first date. Their relationship had blossomed and proceeded without a hitch. Tom had been all of what Sheba wished for and even after three years together Tom still found himself in total awe and fascination of this majestic woman. Sheba was good with his boys, his mother adored her, and she and Zorah got along so well that the two of them arranged most of his son's visitations and outings. Tom and Zorah never ceased having a loving relationship. Neither gave much detail as to the reason for their divorce and when questioned, as if on cue, they'd state "we grew apart". Sheba never pried. She knew her man was a man of integrity and had complete faith in his word. Besides, she had her own suspicions which served her well enough.

After the game the family headed out for their victory dinner.

"35-14, you did good son", Tom said.

"Did you congratulate your brother?", Zorah added.

"I was saving my opinion of his performance until we were alone", Martin said cynically.

"Well, let's hear how proud you are of your brother", Tom said with raised eyebrow and a hint more bass timbre in his voice.

"Well, I was going to tell him that even though I couldn't stop thinking about the animal that was killed or maybe even skinned alive to make the football, I thought he showed great hand to eye coordination...it was like he was one with the tortured animal".

Sheba fought to hold back her laugh.

"And then, I thought about how fast he ran when the coached yelled at him and I said to myself, wow, he doesn't even run that fast to catch the bus to school or when you call him, Daddy...so, I thought Malcolm gave a great performance. I could hear the principal saying, 'run boy, run'.".

"Dad, he's just mad because the chess club doesn't get attention like that. Don't worry Mart, I'll see if I can get some of the lunch ladies to come out and cheer-lead for you next time... HA, HA, HA", Malcolm said with a laugh as boisterous as his father's.

Zorah quickly jumped in and said, "OK OK, you two. You know better. Now shake hands and kiss on the cheek. Now! And tell one another that you're proud of each other". The boys knew they had no choice. Zorah didn't play games. After they made up, the family resumed talking about the game and worked on deciding where they'd have their post-game dinner celebration. They unanimously decided on Indian food. Everyone was mainly vegetarian at this point and only the boys occasionally ate fish or chicken. Zorah and Sheba had launched the campaign to get everyone's diet on point over a year ago. Yes, they were a good team. Sheba felt assured knowing that if she and Tom decided to have a child she already had a good picture of how things would be.

"That was a good visit", Tom said on their hour long drive back home. Sheba agreed. She had always enjoyed getting away from their apartment and spending time with the children. "Zorah's doing such a great job with them. I'm so thankful. When I talk to some of my friends and hear their horror stories I see how fortunate I've been. Zorah and I began as friends and we never played tug of war with the boys. Thank heavens for that. I know Martin had trouble with the change originally but he's adjusted well; all things considered. I'm happy".

Sheba leaned over and kissed Tom on his neck and whispered in his ear "You are a wonderful father and a magnificent fiancée. We're all blessed to have you. I'm especially blessed, my King".

Spencer and Tracey
Verbs of Power

Another fund-raising event perfectly organized by Tracey…

Spencer decided to take a night off from socializing and enlivening the crowd and perched himself near the open bar. Tracey busied herself tending to the details of the gala insuring that the evening continued to progress according to how she planned.

Per Tracey's advice Spencer had been studying for an advanced position at his firm requiring him to take several grueling tests to qualify for consideration. He'd been dragging around for months and that infectious glow in his eyes barely twinkled. For some weeks he had been reflecting on the initial purpose for all of the study and test taking. He worked to place the same level of magnitude on it that Tracey had, but found he felt a bit short-sighted and helpless for not being able to see what she'd seen. It seemed that had always been the nature of the relationship between them.

Just as Spencer began to mentally play out the various outcomes as to how his life would look like after obtaining this new position he was interrupted by a voice.

"Brother, you look really familiar…".

The man responsible for breaking up his thoughts stood in front of him with one eyebrow cocked and a hand on his chin. Spencer said, "Well, I've …uh…worked closely with the foundation for some years now. Actually, my lady put all of this together".

"Nah man, I know you from somewhere else" said the man with a puzzled look on his face before shouting, "Spence!".

"Yes, that's me" said Spencer sitting up in his chair.

"Man, I remember you from the track team; it's me Cordell I used to do the statistics for Coach Moore".

"Cordell, ahh man I remember you. How have you been man? It's been years. I didn't see you at the high School reunion", Spencer said whilst standing up and giving Cordell one of those half handshake hugs that old friends share.

"Man, I've been good" Cordell said pulling up a chair. "Yeah Bro, I couldn't make it. I was in Egypt at the time studying with a group of Kemetologist." Spencer thought to himself,

"What the heck is a kemetologist?" and said, "Oh wow that sounds real cool. I've never been but, always wanted to go. Actually Tracey and I are planning to go to India this year".

"That's peace".

After about an hour of catching up, Spencer found himself revitalized by all the stories and exploits that Cordell shared with him. He learned that Cordell now went by the name Tehuti. Just as Spencer allowed himself to completely emerge himself into this world of history, mysticism, and cultural myth breaking Tehuti said, "Hey man what are you doing this Saturday? Why don't you come down to the liberation bookstore? We have this brother and sister, Nile and Kenya, doing a workshop on economics and sustainability for people of color". Spencer thought, "Why not...anything that'll get me out of spending my Saturday in my office studying". "Sure, I'll see if Tracey wants to go too" replied, Spencer.

Three months had gone by since Tehuti and Spence reunited at the gala. Even though Tracey had yet to attend any of the workshops at the bookstore; Spencer had not missed one since attending the one thrown by Nile and Kenya. Spencer had met some very colorful people at these lectures and loved the way they embraced one another as family. Just as in all other environments he graced, he was able to charm those in his vicinity but, he found that this new information did not come as quick and easy to him as other things in his life. He often considered this was because of the absence of Tracey in this endeavor. Spencer assumed that, without her, his brain just did not function as efficiently as when he was with her. Tehuti told him that coming into "knowledge of self" was difficult for everyone at first because there was so much programming to break through in order to actually begin to be a student. Spencer, for the first time in his life, had truly felt passion. His first reaction to what he had been learning had been utter astonishment, which transformed into hurt, then anger. Spencer had never been angry at anyone or anything in his entire life and certainly not as a result of learning. All the same he felt something pulling and tugging at him to continue learning more.

Spencer had spent many an evening attempting to share what he was learning with Tracey but, never could seem to articulate these new theories and concepts well enough to convey them to her competently. The discussion usually ended with Tracey as the victor. She stated she could appreciate the information but, would often speak about how African-Americans needed to think more realistically. "Black consciousness does not pay the bills Spence", she'd always say. Somehow Spencer knew that there was a direct correlation between knowing your history and economics but, he hadn't internalized these concepts long enough to actually assert this idea. So for now, this was his journey to go through, without Tracey. He hated not being able to enjoy the process with Tracey but, was unwilling to abandon what he'd been learning.

MARRIAGE
You define it, there are no rules.

The proliferation of culturally torn homes has become a divisive chasm that leads to a twisted view of true sacred union. This enemy of matrimonial unity is not as foreign as we'd like to believe. Just as OUR research of any given subject should be approached scientifically from the internal to the external, so should the resolution of our issues be addressed from within, first. No one arrives to this reality with the sole/soul purpose of spending decades trying to figure out how to get along with one person. This is an insane conception but, sadly the most often seen in relationships…even those intimate relationships mistakenly believed to be "good" ones (which are usually just coined that because of the amount of time they last).

It's imperative to ask oneself why "marriage" is seen as an expectant outcome of a harmonious, or disharmonious, relationship. This robotic procession to a thoughtless soul binding does not take into account that marriage does not stave relationship challenges but, on the contrary, amplifies them. The decision to proceed to spiritual union should be made consciously and not because of what seems to be a societal urging due to the amount of time you've spent with the person you're currently with or some unseen "biological clock". Also, marriage should not be used as a bargaining chip or as a cure-all for relationship issues.

There's a multi-generational perpetuated mass idea that states marriage is a narrow-minded uniform institution of only one design and format. This book is not about the multitude of marital formats implemented throughout the globe from time immemorial so, I will say it's best to find a format that works best for you and your partner and refine it to your combined needs and imperatives.

A spiritual union rooted in true admiration, raspect, and constructive intention will insure civility and like-mindedness during a committed relationship….and in the event, divorce.

<u>CHILD REARING</u>

Children do not come from us; they come through us.

When individuals choose to have children in a slapdash manner with anyone who will provide an egg or sperm, without objectively considering the integrity or character of the person desired to co-create with they are playing a game of Russian roulette with the lives of future children. A child has a divine right to manifest the highest or lowest nature of the mother, father, a combination of them both, or their environment. This should be solemnly considered when one is looking to procreate with their current or idealized partner. There are instances where a child will physically, emotionally, or mentally exhibit the traits of one parent to a "T", regardless of the rearing they've received. This, in most cases, cannot be trained or "disciplined" out of them. This is why family backgrounds should be thoroughly researched and uncovered.

All too often one parent will make a pronounced cultural investment and the other parent makes a choice, informed or uninformed, to choose a lifestyle or culture that sits in direct opposition to their parental counterpart. This scenario causes a "split camp" and a home with a spirit of multiple personality disorder.

This author does not advocate any form of religious or social indoctrination for children as this only creates a ceiling of awareness development crowned by their parents own ceiling of conscious awareness. Instead, I advocate a doctrine of exposure and experience for children in order to objectively allow them to see the immensity of life for themselves as opposed to developing a culture of rules and fear that they'll have to combat in their latter years. This needs to be agreed upon, jointly, by all parents involved in the child rearing process. If that does not happen children could choose to rebel from the familial norms and mores all together. This is a predestinated ensnarement that many families fall into.

Our children and mates are, often, the only ones on the planet that can bring us to our lowest of lows or highest of highs. They are typically the reasons for our greatest sacrifices; which links us to them in greater measure compared to those we choose to associate with without altering much of ourselves. With that in mind parents should design the proper scenario for children to emerge from. Simply put, children should be planned. Discussions surrounding child rearing should occur during the courting stage. This is just one of the reasons for a properly designed courting routine. There's nothing worse than finding out that you and your mate have opposing visions for your progeny after that progeny has been created. To this end it's important to research the conditions that each partner was reared under, themselves. Even in cases where an individual decides to make a concerted effort to improve or, counteract, their own childhood whether, dysfunctional or functional, it's still key to be made aware of what the childhood consisted of in terms of parental techniques and rearing methodologies. More often than not, the Mango does not fall far from the roots.

THE EVOLUTION

Nile and Kenya
The Hand of the Elders

"Sure Baba, I can be there at that time. Whatever is most convenient for you. I'll be there. OK, O'Dabo". Nile settled further into his recliner chair and took a moment to center his thoughts reflecting on the contribution he and Kenya had made over the past year to the ongoing pro-comeunity effort. Through their efforts they'd actually been able to increase the clientele for their own individual businesses. The young doctor had one of the most prosperous years in his entire practice and Kenya had recently been commissioned to provide translation services for a popular West African author so that his works could be enjoyed by Africans within the Diaspora. They'd truly been able to take one another to another level.

An hour later Nile was sitting in the Freeman family library exchanging pleasantries and catching up on small talk.

"Things have been going well for you Nile. I've heard some wonderful things. I tell everyone about how you got me back on track. What you've done for me, alone, still amazes me."

"I just assisted the process your body had already begun, Baba. You have a strong mental constitution so; you didn't fight the process or expect unearned results. That kind of brings me to the reason I came here today."

"I'm all ears. What's on your spirit Nile?"

Nile breathed deeply and began to tell Baba Freeman what he'd known he'd have to lay on his shoulders for the past month. Nile stroked his beard and leaned forward towards Baba Freeman as the older man instantly leaned in and turned his head, with ear facing Nile, in order to intensify his listening.

"I feel that we can speak openly, Baba. Since we've been working together to maintain your health at a state of normalcy, I've come to observe your ritualistic habits you employ to govern your well-being. I gained great admiration and reverence for you and Mama Freeman as well as the Ma'atic sanctity of your home."

Baba Freeman's look waned increasingly somber but, remained stoically unreadable. He sat still providing his undivided attention and focus to Nile so as to fully absorb what he shared via his spoken word.

"If you're open and consenting to it, I'd like to approach sister Kenya with a proposal for courtship and I wish for you and Mama Freeman to oversee it", Nile nervously said with his hawk like gaze scanning the older Jegna. Nile leaned back slightly in his chair he was sitting in and shifted his weight so that he could produce the implied psychological effect of space so as to not crowd Baba freeman or make him feel rushed, though he doubted that was accomplishable.

After an extended period of silence Baba Freeman simply said, "Are you hungry, son?". Before Nile could respond, Baba Freeman called out to Mama Freeman and asked if she'd seat a place for Nile. Nile taken aback fidgeted in his chair but remained speechless and compliant.

Two hours after eating a delicious meal and helping Mama Freeman clean up the kitchen Nile took out the household trash. Baba Freeman then brought three ripe mangoes and beckoned for everyone to sit in the family room to enjoy the tasty dessert. Upon finishing Nile, still preoccupied with the purpose for his visit, tried his best not to seem anxious. Luckily, before any uncomfortable silence could develop, Baba Freeman turned to him and said, "What are your intentions towards Sister Kenya post courtship?". In a flash Nile stated, unblinkingly, "I intend to create a family with her".

"Do you desire to have children with her and if so, how do you plan on providing for them?"

"Yes, I would love to co-create with the sister. As far as supporting my family, I'm currently in the process of partnering up with another holistic healer to expand into the arena of teaching for additional revenue. We'd be teaching the holistic medicinal arts and providing certification. I've been sharpening my outdoor survival skills, martial sciences, building and home maintenance, and I've recently purchased a used spare car to practice my automotive mechanics. Right now, I've got my eye on a fourteen acre plot of land thirty miles up country that I plan on using to build a self-sufficient homestead. This space will also serve as the location for the school. I've been studying green building techniques and have already secured financing for the materials and crew. These are some of the steps that I've taken to insure financial freedom for my family and maintain/

protect what I do provide. I want to make sure I have the skill and ability to protect what we build together, and preserve our possessions. I also have intensified my cultural studies so that I can have something of worth to teach our future children".

Slowly, Baba Freeman turned to face Mama Freeman and as though they telepathically exchanged unverbalized thoughts, Mama Freeman turned to Nile and said, "You've put some commendable mechanisms in place but, what have you done to guarantee this family doesn't begin to feel like a machine or just another strategized accomplishment?"

"I have come to realize...or rather feel a great deal of chemistry between Kenya and myself. I am enamored with her and though I know the relationship must make sense, I certainly have developed an immense measure of affection and fondness for her. We have become genuine friends and partners in our work. I know we have great respect and admiration for each other as individuals. I like how I feel when I'm with her and feel that what we are together needs to be reproduced for the good of the community."

"OK, that barely answers my question, honey. You've done the planning and you've calculated the mathematical equations in regards to you and Kenya. What is the source of your attraction?".

With a bit of discomfort Nile admitted, "I've never met a wombmyn as magnificent as her, inside and out, although I don't want that to be my paramount motivation...she is absolutely beautiful". Nile paused and rubbing his hands together narrowed his eyes and said, "I don't know all I need to know. I recognize I've put a lot of linear thought into all of this but, perhaps there's a greater emotional intelligence I need to gain. I'm open to learning whatever I need to. Kenya is dear to me and I'd like to be the best man, not the best person, I have the potentiality to be for her and what we produce." Nile then decided to take a daredevil leap of faith and poised the question "Will you help me?"

Mama Freeman turned to Baba Freeman and although her mouth seemed fashioned into a faint smile, Nile was not at all sure of their reaction to his proposal. He could hardly discern the vibes between the three of them due to the pounding of his own heart. Mama Freeman then placed her hand over Baba Freeman's hand, turned to Nile and placed her hand at Nile's temple, completing the circuit. She closed her eyelids and held this position for what seemed like an hour but, was probably more like ten minutes. During this time Nile could feel her probing his mind and spirit. Nile struggled to clear his head.

Osunsina Freeman was a powerful spiritual consultant, spiritual guide, and "Iya" to many of Nile's associates. The Elder wombmyn was no joke. Nile noticed Mama Freeman was now squeezing Baba Freeman's hand and the Elder man was nodding his head knowingly. Nile wondered what was being exchanged in their private language. Mama Freeman then broke the circuit and opened her eyes. Nile looked between the two of them and was overcome with an insurmountable feeling of awe. Baba Freeman turned to fully face Nile and said. "We'll do this together contingent upon Kenya's approval."

"Juicy, sweet, dark, and soft."

As Kenya and Mama Freeman perused the isles of the farmers market, they commented on the plums that had been offered for sampling. "Mmm, I'm going to have to get a few of these along with those peaches for a nice fruit salad", Mama Freeman delightfully exclaimed. As she and Kenya stored their bought goods in the rolling basket Kenya had brought with them, Kenya lamented on the bitter-sweet fact that she had been unable to enjoy these types of moments with her own biological mother. Kenya's mother, by all accounts, was aggressively ignorant. A young Kenya had cured herself of severe asthma at the age of 13 as a result of a personal decision to eat vegan; much to her mother's chagrin. Her mother made it clear, in no uncertain terms, that she loved her DIEt and if she had to she'd "bite a pig on the butt!" Kenya's parents divorced when she was nine years of age and as a result Kenya was forced to adopt an entirely new eating, religious, and social paradigm. Even at three she recalls the digression being awkward. Her father, a notable sculpture artist, demanded that his family eat an eating regiment which he called "I-tal". This consisted of organic vegetables, fruits, whole grains, and plenty of fresh juices. He also required the women in the family to wear their hair naturally and dress modestly; usually with hair wraps and full length dresses. Kenya always remembered the reaction her family would inspire when they strolled together in public. Her parents received so many nods of respect and salutations filled with reverence and admiration. To Kenya's dismay this was short lived. It seemed as though once her parents divided, her mother's devotion to these family customs ended along with the relationship. The baby was thrown out with the bathwater. Kenya took a moment to say a silent prayer of thankfulness for her relationship with Mama Freeman.

"Land my child, land", Mama Freeman said jokingly.

"Huh...oh...I was lost in thought for a moment."

"No, you were up in the clouds, as usual....my little day visionary. You didn't hear a word of what I said, did you?"

"Yes, I did."

"So, then what's the answer?"

Kenya paused for a moment and then slowly said with a raised eyebrow and childish smirk, "Yeah Mama...I have all of her books she died though right?" Kenya and Mama Freeman then burst out in a round of hearty laughter.

"OK, you got me. I was on my cloud sofa again"

"I was asking if you needed to stop home before we met Baba Ola and Nile at the house for dinner."

"No. We can go straight there. These items will keep in the trunk of my car or I'll put them in your basement to stay cool." Kenya felt a sensation of comfort knowing that the Freeman's house was like a home away from home for her.

"That's fine; and by the way you need to buy some more of those black olives", Mama Freeman said walking away.

"Why? I have plent---" Kenya looked down at the plastic bin of what were olives in her hand and realized that she was so lost in thought that Mama Osunsina picked and ate her olives right out of her hand leaving only the pits. Kenya thought, "Serves me right. She does this every time. I really love her...". Kenya expressed another thought of appreciation directly to the soul of Mama Freeman for the constancy between them.

Once they arrived at the homestead they were greeted by Baba Freeman who promptly walked to the driveway and relieved the car of its burdens and took them indoors. Entering the kitchen, Baba Freeman informed them that Nile would be along later in the evening. He shot a knowing look at Mama Freeman and by intimate syncopation she beckoned them to all have a seat in the study. Without wasting any time Mama Freeman turned to

Kenya and said, "Dear, we have some news to share with you. I will tell you and provide you with a moment to think and then respond...".

Kenya replied, "OK, I'm all ears".

"It has come to our attention that there is a young man who has taken a great interest in you and desires to spend time with you in hopes to build a familial relationship. Would you be interested?" Kenya's heart sank into the soles of her feet, which were now numb and cold along with her fingers. She was not un-accustomed to the advances of men and had, overtime, learned she carried a certain appeal that men found desirable but, this felt sudden. She knew this was a proposition that was to be taken seriously because if these Elders were approached by a poten-tial suitor, and they saw fit to bring this to her attention this all had come as a result of much scrutiny and screening performed by these wise ones. She did not want to foolishly turn away the possibility of partnering with a good mate as she held her own longing for family but, her heart was leading her in a course that she'd been perfectly content with.

Kenya asked, "Who is this person?"

"Now is not the time to reveal that. It could lead to a pos-sible conflict and discomfort between you two. What is most needed, right now, is for us to know if you're open to the idea and if your spirit is leading you this way. I would not want you to be distracted by anything you may or may not think you know or believe about this brother but, you know I love you as my own blood child and would never involve you in any situation that is incorrect", Baba freeman said sternly but, with a gentleness of tone.

"I know, Baba Ola". Kenya breathed deeply and closed her eyes. She placed her right hand over her heart while circu-larly stroking her left hand over her abdomen. She then opened her eyes after half-a-minute and said with conviction, "Yes, I'd like to meet the brother".

"My baby girl, always the cautious one", Mama Freeman said while wrapping an arm around Kenya and kissing her fore-head. She then whispered "I wish you and Nile the greatest of fortune. He's earnest and you are precious." Kenya smiled the widest smile she had in years and embracing Mama freeman al-lowed their tears of joy to commingle as her fears dissipated and her vision materialized.

Spencer and Tracey
Called and Chosen

"I give honor to my Ancestors; those on whose shoulders I stand. I come to the house of my Ancestors with an offering of cool water. I ask that we strengthen one another for the journey that calls to us both. Ase." Spencer knelt before his grandparent's headstone in tranquil rumination. He gave thought to the countless forgotten and neglected Ancestors whom nested in his family tree. He'd meditated, as he did every Sunday during his Ancestral ritual, on the significance of his own birth. At one time what seemed so random to him now conjured images of celestial genetic engineering. He realized that he came to the planet to advance the outstretching limbs of his own family tree further towards the blinding unknown bounds of the Sun. In reality, Spencer never felt more relevant than now. Looking across the endless sea of headstones he viewed them as ancient stone cherubim marking the way to the ancestral webs of wisdom for mortals still in search of the unseen truth. His new set of customs and practices had become an intense yearning in his heart. Spencer knew the universe had a story to be told and he planned on being a co-author and an illiterate passive victim of ignorance no longer." I am the co-author of my own life destiny", whispered Spencer. "I ask for enlightenment and protection for all of my loved ones. Lead us all into the actualization of our greatest selves. I ask that my unborn child guide me and show me patience. Protect my home and stabilize my---" **HONK!!! HONK!!!** Spencer swung around quickly and saw Tracey in the passenger seat of his vehicle offering only her side profile in view as she faced the windshield of the truck. With her sunglasses on Spencer could read no sign of immediate agitation on her face but, certainly sensed it. Spencer proceeded to light incense at the tomb of his grandparents and positioned a bouquet of flowers. He felt the presence of his grandmother wrap his head in what felt like velvet.

"Thank you, Nana, for your love and direction. I will do all I can to serve you to the best of my ability. I know you've been guiding me all along and you have whispered words of peace and wisdom to us all. Please continue to---"
HOONNK!!!!! HOOONNNNK!!!!!!!HOOONNNNKK!!!!!!!
Spencer spun around this time to see Tracey with her sunglasses

raised on her forehead and a look of impatience and agitation while she pointed to her watch contorting her face into the most wretched of disfigurement. Grabbing his belongings and quickly saying goodbye to his spirit guardians, he briskly jogged to his vehicle with a feeling of levity and grace.

"I mean Spencer come on. This is why I told you to meet me at the house after you finished your prayer thing.", Tracey said cynically with a mocking quotation used with her middle finger and index fingers of left and right hands when she worded "prayer thing".

"Tracey, I was hoping you would have gotten out of the car this time and greeted my grandparents", Spencer lamented.

" Spence, I'm not into all of this. I'm a Christian and you know that...we were baptized together. I was hoping you'd re-member your roots and realize the times have changed. It's like you're just so lost, lately."

"Trace, my roots are what this is all about. Babe, what were we before our Ancestors were slapped in the face with Bibles and our babies stomped into the soil by the boots of cross wearing Christian slave-makers? You know our history lives before the 1600's..."

"Yeah Spence, and it's just that, history. I am a proud black woman but, I don't have to do all of that hoodoo-voodoo to prove it to myself or anyone else."

"True, you don't have anything to prove...only a lifetime of programming to decode and reckon with".

"Aren't you the wise one now. Not too long ago you could have cared less about an Ancestor or Mama A-free-cuh..."

As Spencer navigated his way through the winding cem-etery path he felt anger, embarrassment, and the egoistic pull of a challenge rushing through his veins like a roaring monsoon. "OK Tracey...no need to argue. Let me just ask you this; have you ever asked yourself why you are here...questioned the meaning of your existence?"

"Oh please Spencer", Tracey snorted and put her sun-glasses over her eyes placing her delicate foot on Spencer's dash-board while fiddling with the climate controls.

"I know it's tough, brother, a prophet has no honor in his own home", Tehuti said comfortingly as Spencer explained his frustration at the increasing frequency of disagreements he was experiencing with Tracey.

"Yeah I've heard this before but, I mean...How can one turn from what makes the most sense and choose something that is insane? I find it hard to believe that if we present a glass of clean water and one with dirty water that the filthy water will be chosen. I know I'm not crazy."

"No, you're not crazy my brother but, just because you've learned some things doesn't mean that people are now obligated to respect your opinions, findings, or you. The journey can be a very lonely one at times, Spence....I've told you that. There may come a moment when you'll be forced to decide between freedom or bondage to social attachments. This is your life purpose and in the end your perspective of truth may hold reason for you and you alone". Spencer thought about all of the years he and Tracey had spent together and failed to imagine a future without her. The thought scared him. Tracey was his rock; his source of strength and courage. Tehuti interrupted his mentation with a jarring accusatory assertion, "Spence your ego has always been your most underhanded adversary".

"Come again?" This statement barely sunk in as Spence knew himself to be humble and receptive despite what his social status ever implied.

"What I'm saying is you assume you've come into this new awareness of yourself by some haphazard chance occurrence. You forget the Ancestors are always masterminding and conspiring to bring out your superior potential. Your self-importance gives you the illusion of separation from your root of luminance. You were predestined to learn these lessons, my brother. You were chosen and all of your steps and missteps were meant to bring you right to this place of learning and doing, baptized in the clean water that you speak of. Be grateful for being one who was called and chosen".

"I didn't look at it like that", Spencer said with soft approval. He felt a sudden rush of responsibility but, was puffed up with the love he felt as a result of being chosen." I've made plenty of space in my life for Tracey to function freely but now I'm feeling like this calling, as you call it, should be treated with more honor than I've given. Tracey has been like a bull unleashed in a crystal shop. I have a lot to think and lay on at my shrine".

"I have faith in you", Tehuti said planting a firm hand on Spencer's shoulder although Spencer seemed so deep in thought he didn't even respond to Tehuti.

"Spencer, Spencer, Spence!"
"Huh? Oh...thanks babe." Spencer was deep in thought and Tracey's attempts to pass the plate she had just prepared for him hadn't even been heard amongst the voices of reasoning in his own mind. It was the annual "Thanksgiving" dinner that Tracey and Spencer's families had jointly celebrated ever since any of them could remember. "What's going on with you today? You've been in *la-la land* since this morning".
"Oh, me? I'm cool. I guess just a little tired, is all".
"Well, after this meal I'm sure you'll fall right out in front of the football game same as every year", Spencer's mother said to the amusement of all at the table. Spencer laughed half-heartedly and said, "Maybe I'll drink some of this ginger beer Aunt Mimi sent to keep me up long enough to see Dad's team lose". Everyone laughed while Spencer's father flashed a mock warning glare around the table. Spencer, although in an unusually pensive mood, couldn't help but feel the warmth and contentment this day carried for him. He only wished that his family was more accepting of the life choices he'd been slowly making. Then they would all be thankful as one.
Surprisingly his mother had shown great interest in some of the information he'd been acquainting himself with and had even taken him to the attic storage some months back to share books on transcendental meditation, world religions, politics, and her prize possession....a huge photo collection of her, in her much younger years, as a relief worker in Kenya, Ethiopia, and Eritrea. His mother had shared that during these times she'd aspired to work as a minister of cultural affairs in an African country. "Sure, back in those days I had far reaching dreams to go to the Motherland and help build a nation, any nation, to a place a prominence". Spencer's mother, endearingly known as "Sister" to everyone, had been one who typified the role of Mother and wife although she was a college graduate who held a masters degree in Community Planning and Administration; she'd only worked short-term consultant contracts from time to time. Spencer knew his mother to be highly intelligent but, her intellect and

creativity was utilized for the development and support of her husband and four children. During their attic journey through the halls of nostalgia Sister revealed that she never forsook her desire to do some good for her people, here and abroad. She'd made the decision to focus her efforts on her immediate family and help grassroots organizations whenever she could. There was one photo album, which revealed a much more intriguing story about this complex mother of his than Spencer had ever expected to uncover. In one photo album sister held a photograph of her and a much younger, slimmer, and vibrant image of a man Spencer knew well; Tracey's father "Big Henrik". There were photographs of the two of them working political campaigns, marching, decked out in African clothing, handing out books and fliers, distributing breakfast to young children, and even cleaning parks. "I never realized you and Big Henrik went this far back. I've never seen pictures this far back of you, even with dad."

"This was before I met your father. Henrik and I were quite a pair. We were determined to change the world or at least leave our marks. Those were very exciting times back then and we worked well together soaking it all up. We met at a student rally, actually. Henrik threw himself into a police officer to prevent the cop from arresting me. I bailed him out afterwards."

"You arrested? I can't even imagine it."

"No need to, it's all right here", she said defiantly while reaching deep into the trunk that held the unspoken past she'd never shared until this day. Sister produced a scrapbook full of pictures and newspaper clippings. In one picture, in particular, Spencer saw his dear mother scraping the face of a police officer with one hand while grabbing his baton with the other. She held the most vicious battle ready look he'd ever seen. As he read further, he saw a list of the people arrested at a student protest and in clear print saw his mother's name. Spencer's jaw dropped as he peered in disbelief at the pictures and read that his mother had been arrested during a student uprising. "Back then we were well trained. I only made it up to green belt in Jiu-Jitsu but, I was something else", Sister whispered with great undulation. Henrik was not only a massive intellectual who was engrossed in the issues that we face but, he also knew his way around a boxing ring. Just to think...". Spencer saw his mother slightly shaking with excitement and the tone of her voice revealed she had placed herself in that time and place spiritually and mentally and loved every moment of it.

"So, how did it all...um...end for you? I mean what made you..."

"Become a boring homemaker?"

"No! Well, sort of."

"My son sometimes you come to a pivotal moment when a choice has to be made."

Spencer thought to himself, 'doesn't this sound familiar...'

"OK", Sister said exhaling and dropping her head indicating to Spencer she was about to explain in detail what he'd been asking. "Henrik and I, along with many other brothers and sisters, were getting the work done, bottom line. We were mainly working at a grassroots level but, felt the best way to change certain institutions and strongholds was by changing the policies that affected us all. Many in our group disagreed and said they were unwilling to compromise or water down their positions on certain issues. Henrik would debate the only way we'd be able to affect long term change was to weave ourselves into the very fabric of the strongholds we were battling and change them from within'. Henrik then decided to shed his WARdrobe of opposition for a look and image that would make him much more approachable. He certainly had the ability to navigate any social rung he wanted. He went into the corporate sector and even joined various high society organizations. I remained with our comrades but, truthfully, didn't desire to work where Henrik wasn't. I mean I typically took my lead from him. So, eventually I began to escort him to political networking events. I called it information gathering...I suppose that was to placate my ever growing sense of guilt for leaving the front-line work. As time passed it became less and less about the impending social issues and more about achieving a sense of personal success in order to be the examples of accomplishment we felt our people really needed. We convinced ourselves that we should be the sacrificial lambs offering our blatant and overt community activity at the altars of assimilation. Well, eventually Henrik met Anita at a street renaming event that he was covering for the community newsletter. They were slow in coming together but, she was determined" Sister said with a hint of bitterness. Spencer noted it.

"She actually introduced me to your father. I was told years later, years after they were married, that she always had concerns that I'd drag Henrik back to his former life of "crime" because, I had his ear like none other". Spencer remained silent. "Well, your father and I met and he made it clear that nothing was more important to him than family and after we married and raised our children we could both go on to pursue what he called our dreams. I remember one day showing him my pictures and he told me it's good to have a hobby as long as it doesn't become an obsession."

"Why didn't you go back to your mission once we were all grown and out of the house", Spencer inquired.

"Mission...." Sister smiled at the words as it left her lips. "People are different now, son. Henrik has his family and work, and I'm too old to go marching in the streets beatin' up cops", the loving woman said with a chuckle while playfully ringing Spencer's neck.

"No, really Mother. I think what you were doing is important and is still needed. This is your life journey. No one else co-signs it but, you. Even if you're alone in your struggle, it should never be discredited because of that." Spencer then let out a laugh and slapped his knee.

"What's so funny?"

"I just realized the meaning behind a lesson a friend was trying to share with me."

"You know what Spencer? "

"What?"

"I'm proud of you, and you're right." Sister stood up and kissed her son on the head. "Now Spencer, what will you do?"

"Huh?"

"I said, what will you do?", Tracey questioned again.

"About what?"

"What will you do with all the money from your new promotion?"

"Oh, that. I haven't given it much thought, Trace. What do you think I should do?"

"Probably wouldn't be a bad idea to now expand and diversify your stock portfolio; maybe even look into some investment property", Tracey said instructively but, unforced.

As they jogged along the wooded path, both in perfect sync, Spencer used the time to organize his thoughts. The past few months he'd felt such inner warfare. Spencer focused his efforts on gaining the much needed job promotion that required less travel allowing him to devote more time to his studies. Spencer typically enjoyed jogging in silence. It seemed the only time, as of late, he and Tracey could remain in agreement for an extended period was when they jogged. Tracey had been overly talkative this afternoon and Spencer felt it important to give her this ear time. Spencer hadn't been his usual light-hearted self since the talk with his mother in his parent's attic. Something had been triggered in him making him more fearful than ever before. He'd even experienced a few nightmares with the consistent theme of him being set adrift in a rubber raft in the middle of a vast body of water or trekking through a desert alone feebly climbing massive dunes. He'd wake up with his heart racing clutching for Tracey in the middle of the night. As they slowed down their pace and ended their run at the boat docks they began to stretch one another out.

"Tracey?"

"Yeah, babe?"

Spencer held Tracey's legs on his shoulder and was watching her press her forehead to her knee. "You ever think what it would be like if we weren't together?"

"Sure", Tracey said flatly not even noticing the look of hurt on Spencer's face as she changed legs. When she noticed his body stiffing she said, "Spencer we used to play in the crib together and we've known each other before we even knew our own genders. I had girlfriends in college who shared their stories of dating a bunch of different guys and I was curious at times but, that's all; nothing more. I always knew what you and I have is rare and it makes more sense than anything else I've ever been a part of. Inwardly, Tracey hoped this statement could contribute to the peace needed as a result of the recent onslaught of disagreements.

"And you?"

"Honestly, I've never even liked anyone else. Sure, I saw females who caught my eye but, I didn't feel anything for any of them. With you, I always could be myself." "Up until recently", Spencer thought to himself but, his pause revealed this though and Tracey knew she needn't pry. All of a sudden Spencer felt a sensation of urgency rush over him and for some reason he needed to end this incertitude he held with regard to Tracey. He sensed their relationship had been a product of chance and maybe even family arrangement/coaxing. As Tracey cupped the nape of Spencer's neck with both of her hands and pulled his head towards her chest, she said with slight trepidation "What's wrong Spencer? You're holding back." Spencer grabbed both wrist of the petite woman, looked up at her, and with tears in his eyes peered into her own and finally demanded something of Tracey which he knew would arrest the mounting division in their relationship.

"What?", Tracey asked incredulously.

"I said, marry me."

<u>DIVORCE</u>

Divorce has long been a, sometimes abject, destination of male/female disunity. If there is a terrible misunderstanding surrounding the true nature of "marriage", certainly the same could be said for divorce and separation. Divorcing from a conceptual union or relationship (all relationships are merely a web of intent, concepts, and connections) should not become a campaign of exposing villainy and hatred in your previous mate but, should be performed as respectfully as the process of ceremonially coupling. There can be many reasons to separate from a previous life partner but, the obligatory gift of tending to one's family, even through the transmutation of divorce, should never be abandoned. If family is a web of connected ideas and spiritual ritual then, one should let the idea of what is/was evolve. The nature of the relationship should simply change, not pervert and implode into confusion. Never suffocate the rootage and foundational purpose of family. In doing this you choke out the life of your community. Community is the next step from family. Retarded family, active or post-marital, begets a retarded community.

When infatuation, possession, and obsession serve as fuel for your union consequently those very same energies will dominate the post-breakup climate. These types of emotions keep your soul-connected to an individual that you may need to break from if the relationship was not a fortuitous one. Consider the genesis of these emotions and impositions. Realize that projecting any of these feelings towards an individual is the beginning of co-enslavement. True love and unity loses itself in this type of environment.

Divorce should not be a precursory declaration of war. When it is, not only is the hearts and minds of the former couple thrashed about and damaged, the products of those couplings; which are most often children, are thrust into a gladiator arena of hostile human affairs. Children are trapped in a torrent of emotional torture and emotional insanity when their adult parents refuse to function in their sacred roles as caretakers and guides. Unfortunately, there are times when one parent must intensify their work as protectorate when needing to protect their offspring from their parental counterpart.

Solutions for Dysfunctional Family Relationships

There are some things to consider when contemplating divorce:

1. How will this divorce affect my family and subsequently my community?
2. Is the reason for this divorce based on factors that are in alignment with my own personal convictions or am I following someone else's standards?
3. How will my children perceive marriage and divorce as a result of this?

When divorce is a product of an unequal coupling consideration, regard for one another's process of improvement should be in place, unceasingly. If one-half of a former union finds themselves further along on the road of knowledge, wisdom, and innerstanding than their former counterpart; license is not automatically issued to behave harshly with the mate who is less developed. In fact, if one finds that they are further along or more "in the know" than their current or ex-partner, then ethically the burden of accountability, maturity, obligation, and peaceful resolution lies on them. Heightened awareness is a responsibility. One should not attempt to use their "consciousness" as a tool for oppression, brow beating, or tyranny. Be kind to the growing mind. This is not to say underdevelopment provides one with a free pass to savagery and thoughtlessness. All contributing parties should always be held accountable for their actions as should societal influences, socially engineered oppressive agendas, extended family, family friends, and children.

THE REAPING

Tom and Sheba
The Dancing Child

Sheba sat on the park bench reading her book on pre-natal nutrition while running her fingers across her belly in the warm sunlight. In her pocketbook she kept the pregnancy test that she'd taken only a few days ago still displaying the"+" diagnosis. Still unsure of her exact date and time of conception, she knew she'd been considerably late on her monthly cycle and this was a rarity. As Sheba read through the book that had been stored on her shelf for several years the words seemed to leap off the pages in a way that they'd never before. Now, facing this new chapter in her life caused the chapters in her book to garner an entirely new relevance and authoritative voicing. Sheba had dreamed of having a child of her own for so many years that the moment seemed surreal to her. She enjoyed the time spent with Tom's sons but, was always cautious in reminding herself that they were not her biological children and her clock was ticking away. She knew this may have been of no concern to anyone else other than her so, in this she maintained sight of her original agenda to form her own family unit complete with fruit of her own womb.

Sheba hadn't made Tom aware of this new revelation. They were still preparing themselves for a future life together and hadn't even entered into an engagement yet but, they were both sure that they'd be together for the rest of their lives. Sheba was exhilarated at the news of a new addition but, in the pit of her soul felt a jitter as she hesitated in informing her lover. She had spent over three years with Tom and knew within that she had never rightfully fully uncovered herself to this man. Sheba always figured there'd be time for that when they were married but, in truth, she had maintained her cover for so long she could hardly see the urgency to come clean now. She had more heart to hearts about what she felt was sacred to her with Zorah than she did with Tom. This never bothered her to any great degree until this present moment. Sheba entered a state of lonesomeness at this thought but, also felt guilty for never truly giving Tom the opportunity to know what she knew and "catch up". She vowed, to herself, that she'd remediate this.

Sheba left the park bench and made her way back home

where Tom was preparing dinner for them both. As she entered the front door she prepared herself for what she knew was a long overdue conversation with the man in her life.

"Tom?"

"What's up suga' lips?"

"I was curious, if you had another child would you do anything different this time around?", asked Sheba.

"I've never thought about it much. Taste this and tell me if it needs more curry."

"No, it's perfect. Then, think about it now."

"You mean like in raising them or who I had them with?"

"All of it."

"I guess as far as who I'd have them with....I'd have them with a fine young thang' named Sheba", Tom said while pinching Sheba on her thigh. "As far as raising them...I'd have to say that I'd try to keep them closer to me if I wasn't near their mother. It's rough driving an hour to see the boys sometimes and I'm not able to be close by for emergencies like last year when Malcolm sprained his wrist during that football game. Although, I think the space between Zorah and I helped us to operate a little better because after the divorce we were able to give one another the privacy and distance we both needed to put our lives back together, which I think that actually helped the boys in other ways. Truthfully, I'm pretty happy with the job we both did in the beginning and you've been a tremendous help. I could have never imagined in a thousand years that you would have come in and helped to raise my...the boys like you have. Aside from preparing for the event of divorce, financially, there's not much I would have done differently...maybe I would have given Martin a tougher name."

"Did you ever feel that maybe you could have taught them anything other than what they're learning in school about their origins? To give them a stronger sense of who they are."

"Well, Zorah does Kwanzaa with them and she has them involved in a lot of cultural activities so, we're covered there. I know it's important to her. I've always been a simple type of guy, you know that. I treat people like I'd want to be treated and I keep my heart clean. To me that's what's most important. My boys know they have a father who loves them and works hard to provide for their needs. I make sure we make every family reunion and they've always loved spending time with my parents. I think the rest just kind of works itself out."

"So, you don't feel like a boy should learn about who he is, ethnically, from his father? I mean I know the rites of passage program that Zorah has the boys in teaches them about manhood and culture but don't you feel they should see some of those principles and tenants reflected in or at least taught to them by their own father? Just a question..." Sheba caught herself raising her pitch but, caught herself knowing that she'd have to broach these subjects delicately with forbearance.

"Sounds like these are loaded questions, Sheba. I know you never ask me anything about the children, or future children, without premeditation. What's on your mind love?"

"I've just been thinking lately about what it may look like when or if you and I have a child of our own. You know culture and knowledge of self are very important to me, Tom. I know we don't talk about it much but, learning about who I am as a Black woman changed my life around totally and all of the things that you love about me are mainly a by-product of my Sankofa journey that I took years ago to rediscover my lost self. There's another side to me that I would want my children exposed to."

"Sheba, I'm not going to lie. I'm not all that versed in African culture. I'm open to learning some things but, at the same time, I feel that all civilizations have something to contribute to the advancement of society. I mean there's only one race and that's the human race. I think it's important that we learn how to operate in the global market as opposed to striving for separation. My children will know how to function in today's world. Absolutely, they should learn about the accomplishments of the ancients but, I want them to be able to make a good life for themselves in the here and now."

"It's not about separatism, Tom. It's about identity. We're here and we have to determine our place in the global market but, it's also fundamental to ascertain how we were placed on the soil that we currently stand on. By understanding our past accomplishments it will help our children to know what their historical strengths are. As it is now we already ignorantly associate certain ethnic groups with specific skill sets...Indians with accounting, Jews with business, Asians with manufacturing, Germans with engineering, and so on. What is the African child associated with other than rap music and sports?"

"I understand Sheba. Here's my bottom line, if we have a child one day, I'll leave that stuff to you. If you want me to say something to the kid that you think will help them grow just inform me. I'm open to whatever will work best. When we did the naming ceremony for the boys Zorah walked me through it and it turned out great. We're a team and I don't have a problem taking a back seat when we're dealing with things I don't understand. However you want to do it, sweetheart, is fine with me."

"Well, that's how you work with Zorah now but, I'd like my child to see their father as a leader and inspirer of his family. I want my child to see their father on his throne. I don't have a problem with submitting to wise direction, Tom. What is your vision for your children?"

"My vision? I want my children to be happy; I want them to feel loved, to be successful, and to know the world is their oyster. There's nothing that they can't do despite their race. Sheba, is there something you're not telling me?"

"Tom, you don't seem to get it. I'm saying I think it's important for a man to have a bigger vision for his children other than just keeping them alive and happy. I mean really if that's the case than what separates you from a nanny or any other hired help?", Sheba said exasperatingly. With that Tom placed his cooking utensils on the counter and his eyes began to race back and forth between Sheba's two eyes.

"Sheba, is that how you see me? After all I do for my family, including you? To you...I'm no different than a butler or a chauffeur? You know Sheba you've been dragging around here for the past few weeks and you keep asking me these kinds of questions and let me be honest with you, it's really starting to get under my skin. You're always asking me questions while revealing little of what you're actually thinking. I feel like I'm a gold fish in a bowl half the time."

"Tom, we just think differently, that's all. I just see life as being something worth exploring and living with the knowledge of my beginnings. I don't see this society or all of its contributors as beneficial to us as you do. You teach political science but, do you really teach the science of politics or just the procedural guides for western politics? Have you ever considered that maybe the politics that would work best for African-Americans may be totally different from what works for European-Americans? Do you really see this system working for you? I've seen you fret and worry about staff cut backs on your job and take so much crap that you shouldn't have just so you can maintain your place amongst people who barely respect you. With all that you know about politics, why haven't you gone on to develop your own community? It's because you weren't taught that your people are the founders of civilization. Look, I don't' mean to jump down your throat but, this is important to me."

"Sure, I understand. I'm gonna' go run to the store to get a bottle of wine and when I get back, we'll eat."

"Uh...OK...I'll be waiting for you", Sheba said feeling that perhaps she pushed too far.

While waiting Sheba had an urge to call Zorah and look for a different view.

"Queen, I know we've always respected the boundaries of our individual relationships with Tom but, I could really use your help."

"OK, Sheba what's up?"

"Sis, I'm carrying Tom's child. He doesn't know it yet but, I want to tell him right away."

"What's stopping you?"

"I don't know. I just started thinking about our relationship and...well it's been all that I could have asked for but, I realize that there is a big void. I suppressed a lot of who I am in order to be with Tom. He didn't ask me to but, I just knew he wouldn't' be interested in the things that I'm into as far as my lifestyle choices. It's the reason why I've never gotten rid of my apartment. He's been begging me to move in for over a year now and I won't because that would mean I'd have nowhere to erect my shrines and do my rituals. Tom is a beautiful man but I'm not sure if he has what is needed to actually take the lead or if he even desires to take the lead."

"Yes, Tom is a beautiful soul and I love him dearly. I know you do as well but, you have to ovastand that Tom was raised by his mother with the notion that women are to be served and worshiped point blank. His mother was more concerned with him being happy and safe than actually having to learn to take bumps and bruises so, he developed into someone who nests and keeps his head low as opposed to hunting and exploring.

86

I've spoken about this at length with his sisters."

"That makes so much sense. But, the boys are so into learning and breaking new ground. They're rough and even little Martin is an intellectual pathfinder."

"Queen, I've never spoken to you about why Tom and I split out of respect for him and my children but, now there's another child involved and my sons will, beyond question, be affected by this. I left Tom because I never got enough direction and input from him. I found myself relying on the word of men outside of our home more than I did Tom because, frankly, he rarely had an opinion about anything other than music or food. I'm not saying he's shallow because, he's not he feels and loves deeply but, if I'm going to have to take the lead in everything than I'd rather be with myself or find a more compatible mate. It was hard on me because of my feelings for Tom but, the development of these two kings in training was the most important factor for me to consider in my decision. When it came time to give Malcolm the talk about sex, I had to get his martial arts instructor to sit him down and speak to him because Tom just didn't know how to articulate a perspective that was purely male. He started talking about bees and hummingbirds and Malcolm did all he could to not laugh at him. That was pivotal moment for me. I realized that although Tom is a happy, peaceful, intelligent brother he's like...how can I put it?"

"Like a child who's dancing to music that only he can hear in his head", Sheba blurted out.

"I'd say that's accurate".

"Well, I think I have some better insight. I'm really going to have to accept that Tom will probably not be the strong Kingman that I hoped him to be. I thought maybe just by being around me he'd begin to understand more about culture and how necessary it is but, I think I've made him more comfortable in not changing his disposition by making him think he could remain unchanged and still be with me. In his defense I never bring him around my friends in the conscious community or to any ceremonies. I think part of me was afraid of how I'd be perceived; like if I was with him out of desperation or if I wasn't really down with the culture. Initially I was afraid that I'd scare him away and he'd see me as weird or too much work so, I toned everything down but, deep down it's been festering. This lie that I've been living is going to eat at the nucleus of our relationship if I don't give him full disclosure. Anyway, I don't want to tie you up too long plus Tom should be back from the store any minute. Thank you so much, Sister, for sharing with me. You helped me more than you'll know."

"Anytime, Queen. I love you both, dearly, and want to see you stay together. Oh, I almost forgot...Congratulations!"

"Thanks. Peace."

"Peace."

As Sheba put the phone down she spun around and saw Tom standing in the doorway behind her. He looked as if he'd been impaled by the thorns of hurt and betrayal. She searched her mind as quickly as she could to find words that would remove her from the seat of guilt that she felt sliding beneath her. For a moment they just stared at one another. Tom then took a short breath and said through gritted teeth, "Come on, let's eat".

Tracey and Spencer

Lose some to win some

"Your move"

Spencer studied the chess board in front of him and realized he was actually so disoriented amongst his own chess pieces he'd forgotten his original plan of action. Big Henrik, beyond any doubt aware of this fact, was using this to his advantage and sweeping the bulk of Spencer's pieces off of the chess board. This bout, so far, was shaping up to be a massacre but Spencer, preoccupied with more pressing matters, persevered through the match. After check mating Spencer in three movements Big Henrik began to set the chessboard back up exchanging his white position for Spencer's black.

"Spence, have you ever considered who the most powerful piece is on the board?"

"Never gave it much thought but I always assumed it's the Queen. I mean she's the most mobile player."

"I can tell that's how you feel. When you play you do every, and anything, to preserve your Queen."

"I think you should always conserve your best shot and use it at the precise instance. She's the strongest so strategically she should be used as the deal closer, in a manner of speaking."

"That strategy is about as useful as a pork sausage cart at a Hebrew Israelite convention. Go grab us a couple of beers out the ice box and I'll break it down for you."

Spencer did as he was told and coming back pulled his chair up to the table where he'd lost his chess duel and braced to be taught further. Big Henrik was a man of few words but, the ones he used were always very direct. He had a way of making the complex very simple and seemed to have lived many more lifetimes than his age revealed. He was a man of very sound wisdom and keen observance. Spencer always enjoyed spending time with Big Henrik and became somewhat of a deputized son. He seemed to take more interest in this wise man than his own biological sons did. As Big Henrik put the beer bottle to his mouth and pried off the bottle cap with his teeth he began to deposit a gem of wisdom with Spencer.

"OK, the Queen is a mighty player. That's incontestable. She can move horizontally, vertically, and diagonally. That's all good. But, consider this, what happens if the Queen gets captured?"

"I don't know."

"Nothing. If the peat pickin' Queen gets captured by the enemy, it doesn't mean a darn thing. The game moves forward. The most important piece is not the Queen. The most operative player is the King. If the King is caught, the fight ends. He's the one who should be conserved and protected, to the maximum. Some people play this game in fear that something will happen to the Queen and they'll be at a handicap for the rest of the match. This is untrue. She's a player on the board no different than a pawn or rook. She's there to make sure the King is undefeated, at any cost. When you play with the notion that the Queen is the primary player, you've already defeated yourself."

"I understand. I'm beginning to see where you're coming from."

"I'll give you one more example. Why did Adam eat of the forbidden fruit after Eve?"

"I'd say because once she took it the most natural thing was for him to eat it. We receive our nurturing from a woman so, sustenance that women offer is seldom second guessed. We assume it's innocuous."

"Good answer, but he knew the serpent had coerced her into partaking of the fruit. He also knew that God told him directly that if he ate of the fruit he'd surely die but, when the serpent poetized with Eve she said "lest we die". That means we might die. So, he already knew that Eve didn't know how to follow directions but, she was trying to assert herself as the family head with misunderstood intel."

"So, then why did he do it anyway knowing that he'd die?"

"Because his punk tail was too scared to be alone. He'd rather die with his woman than have faith that God would have just taken another rib out of him and given him a more obedient one. He lacked the testicular fortitude to stay on the higher road."

Spencer reflexively shot a glance at his own groin area and tried to place himself in the goat skin of Adam. It was difficult for him to fathom the credibility of such a story but, as a religious myth he could easily interchange the actors and actresses for his healthier understanding.

"Would any of this have to do with my engagement to Tracey?

"Does it expand there for you? If so, use it", Henrik said with a shrug while moving his pawn forward on the chess board.

"I ask because, you congratulated us but, you haven't told me your feelings. It would mean a lot to me to know your take on it all. I just as well assumed that it's what you all wanted to see happen anyway and it was long overdue", Spencer explained while moving his pawn forward to block the onward advance of Henrik's pawn.

"I've already told you all you need to know. How I feel will hold very little weight in the times to come. How you feel, young man, is what you need to consider with great reflection. Whether you feel dread or brazenness, it's all worth taking a look at. You and Tracey have a long history together and nothing will ever change that but, history is also shaped by the future, and the present. Is the past that you both share reflecting the present that you share now? Do you see your future growth progressing parallel? I've sat back and watched you both grow into fine, respectable adults. I'm proud of you both. But, I've seen you take some new directions recently. I question if you'll have the ability to stand by Tracey if she decides to take some new twist and turns, like you, that are not along or even near your own path. Can you walk unparalleled? Of course this is all rhetoric and more importantly...I need another beer", said the older man while leaping his Knight over one of his pawns into the fighting arena on the board. With that the big man left his stool and headed for the refrigerator. Spencer mulled over the questions and consequences that were placed before him and began to search his heart for verity. He knew that nothing Big Henrik ever said was to be whisked away. Underneath all of the picturesque examples he knew this was a grave warning about something that Spencer would have to flesh out on his own. Situating back into his handcrafted Ashanti stool Big Henrik motioned to Spencer to make his move.

"I think I have some of your allegory figured out.", Spencer said launching one of his Bishops out of the opening made by his previously moved pawn in a position threatening Henrik's knight.

"OK, let's hear it", said Henrik as he advanced another

pawn clearing way for his Queen.

"You're saying a person has to approach their relationships complete in themselves and not look for their partners to validate their own personal purpose. If that's the case you can find yourself going down a road of disappointment. First, you should determine if you and the person are even moving in the same direction to insure unity later on down the path. But, even if that unity is lost you have to be grounded enough within to be cool with that because, at the end of the day it has nothing to do with what you're here to do", Spencer explained while advancing another pawn and clearing a way for his other Bishop.

"But, what is it that you're supposed to get from your alliance with a woman? What should you come with?", Big Henrik questions and simultaneously launches his Queen on a diagonal.

"At the end of the day we're born alone and we'll die alone so, it's not so much about looking for an unending relationship, I think. I would guess that notion came from a time when a wife was considered to be an acquisition no different from cattle or property. Ultimately I, as a man...a King, must be able to draw from my own feminine and masculine sides at will in the event that I am single, for any reason. This will also guarantee that I don't fall into the trap of mating for the sake of finding or completing myself", Spencer launches another pawn forward opening up a pathway to his King.

Henrik uses his previously launched Knight to capture one of Spencer's pawns.

Spencer moves his Bishop forward blocking the diagonal path of Henrik's Queen.

"So how would you deal with the possibility of another man becoming more of an authority in your house than you? You know many women hold more dedication to their religious leaders or even their invisible God's than they do to the man that they lay in bed with every night and send off to work every sunrise. What if that situation befalls your home? What will you do?", Henrik asks as he quickly takes Spencer's Bishop.

Spencer advances another pawn clearing a way for his other Bishop.

Henrik then moves his Knight forward to put Spencer's Queen in jeopardy with one jump move.

Spencer moves his Queen up one diagonal and preps the

Knight to be taken.

Henrik takes Spencer's castle.

Spencer moves his Bishop up one diagonal.

Henrik advances the pawn on his far right forward

"I suppose that would have to be determined early on. The couple would have to find a set of guide-lines or a religion that they both can submit themselves to together and the man in the home would have to serve as a high priest of sorts. So, to answer your question, I'd make sure that I'd monitor my family's interaction with outside influences and would do things to make it clear that we counsel one another internally, first. That would also mean that I'd have to really have a thorough grasp of whatever spirituality we come under, if not than any person or entity could come into the home and cause discord". Spencer uses one of his pawns to take Henrik's Queen.

Henrik moves his Castle forward.

Spencer moves his pawn forward again.

Henrik captures that pawn with is pawn.

Spencer moves his Queen forward right next to that pawn.

"It would seem that this plan of action would be a full-time watchdog duty assignment. While you're busy doing all of this does your wife have any say in her own growth or should she leave all the thinking to you?", Big Henrik queries capriciously and moves a pawn forward to put Spencer's Queen in a position of capture.

Spencer sends his Queen diagonally towards Henrik's King

Henrik moves up to the right one diagonal space.

"No, partners should be formidable all on their own. I suppose if someone were to attach themselves to someone who didn't cause some level of growing pains, they risk getting stuck playing watchdog for the rest of their life. They should be well matched." Spencer advances his Bishop forward, takes one of Henrik's pawns and puts his King in check.

"Check"

"So, you're saying steel sharpens steel?" Henrik moves another diagonal to the right.

"I suppose I am. We should be looking to change one another. Because growth is change. We shouldn't be trying to crystallize one another at some stage in our relationship that either one of us felt was most euphoric." Spencer sends his Queen in direct opposition to the King.

"Check"

"It's like this, if you're unable to properly see the position that each person in your life was sent to you to play, you run the risk of putting the wrong person in place to perform a task they were not naturally assigned to do. This may come from not knowing your own true position. For instance a man can be sent a woman who is united with his life purpose but, he overlooks her because he masochistically thinks whomever he mates with should be at odds with his common purpose so he will be forced to validate himself daily. Then in the course of things he could marry who we'll call this adversary to his inherent ideas. The woman who was his co-contributor could then go on to make the same mistake. Then the children of these two unions would end up missing the advantage of both parents being in agreement. So, at that point one may take on the son of his original proper counterpart as his own and try to instill the lessons in him that he failed to in his own sons as a way of repentance. This was all because he preserved a fantasy of a certain type of Queen in his mind and the influence she'd have on his life".

Henrik retreats his King and is safe for now. No Mate.

"Spencer this is really not a big deal, I don't know why you're making such a stink over this."

"My name is a big deal, Tracey."

"It's a name you've had for three months Spencer. No one is even going to recognize it."

"Tracey, people are going to have to get used to what our family name will be. It's not up to us to accommodate their rigidity".

"What are you talking about our family name? I know you don't expect me to call myself Mrs. Krazy Shocklatte!"

"My name is Kwesi Sangolode. I've told you this before and besides do you expect my children to inherit my slave name? Tracey, if we're going to do this there's going to be some changes that we'll both have to adjust to."

"Spencer nothing needs to change other than what is acceptable. I want a fulfilled life and I want us both to grow but

94

there needs to be mutual respect. You never asked how I felt about changing your name, let alone having to change mine to one that no one will even be able to pronounce. Did you consider how I'd feel? I've spent my entire career making a name for myself and you expect me to just start over?"

"But, if I was to take on a name that doesn't speak to my own origins; one that is more socially conforming, you wouldn't be saying this".

"What can I say Spencer? I like conformity. I like order and I don't feel a woman should have to lose her identity just to have a family. I think you're being a bit chauvinistic Spencer."

"Tracey, this can't be all about maintaining what we think we've built because, most of that is illusion and non-investment in our own true survival. It's not about your supposed identity. It's about us finally, having something to reclaim as our own. We are both losing and gaining in getting married. Can't you see that?"

Tracey and Spencer argued for several hours more over which name would be printed on their wedding invitations. As usual it ended with Spencer grabbing his keys and heading out to reason with Tehuti. Midway on his way to Tehuti's storefront he decided to head over to the cemetery and spend some time communing with his Ancestors.

Nile and Kenya
Paradise Lost

*I long for the peaceful place of calm breezes where I'll always find you
Ready to receive my weary body and heal me with your sweet waters
You are the touch that incites me beyond the mundane and leads me to
Zion; moving through moist soil to be the light at the center of earthly
core
I search my own soul and see you. I seek the song of my own heart and
hear your voice beckoning me to vacate my peak and flow into your
valley
I am becoming we majestically*
-Nile

---

*I can have a bit of difficulty expressing my feelings at times so, I've dis-
covered that I respond best to a mate who's patient and willing to learn
unconventional and diverse forms of communication.
I also have challenges with time orientation so, I'm working on being
more punctual.
I can be a little excessive with my wardrobe. I appreciate exquisite fabrics and choice garments and have become somewhat of a collector, although I wouldn't consider myself a hoarder because I do wear everything I purchase.
I'm repulsed by backbiting and gossip.
I've found too many men who can recite ancient verses and breakdown
the symptoms of systematic oppression but, can't change a tire or use
a power drill. I am most secure with someone who has at the very least,
mastered the basics.
Freedom is important to me. I, honestly, don't like being told what to do
and really don't see any reason why anyone should have to come under
anyone else's authority. I know this would lead to social chaos but, in-
nately I feel that if people are left alone to do what they desire nature will
bring order. I'm also working on this perspective.*
-Kenya

"As we have deduced through our process, Kenya you are
one who operates mainly through abstract concept and Nile you
are one who favors the linear approach. With that in mind we'll
analyze your two declarations now. Let's begin to sort through

the information", said Baba Freeman. "Nile, your challenge was to write a profession to Kenya using language which represented the polar inverse of your usual communication modality...something that would take you outside of your comfort zone but, represented what you felt is most receptive to Kenya. Through what you've read to us it's clear that you desire to find a release in life; a way to decline all duty and obligation. You're over worked. In your mate you want to find the one person with whom you can vacate all of your seriousness and receive the nurturing you urgently yearn for. You are also sexually repressed but, this repression comes from attachments to formality that only hold value to you alone. This is why your poem speaks mainly of solitude and carefree excursion. You see your relationship as your salvation but, what you must learn is to treat yourself more tenderly. Your mate will follow your example of how you deal with yourself whether it is a wholesome or unwholesome one. You also show that you are excited about joining with Kenya and creating a working unit."

"Kenya, conversely your task was to represent yourself in a way outside of your comfort zone and speak directly to what your pet peeves as well as turn-ons are in a clear manner; again much unlike your usual lyrical, and even cryptic, way of dialogue. Kenya, you being a linguist who avowedly has trouble expressing your feelings represents an interesting paradox. You translate for others and use clothing to make an expression but, in fact, hold your own thoughts and sentiments guarded close to you. This comes as a result, or at least as a partial by product, of the disappointments you've experienced with different men. If you have an understanding of what the basic responsibilities of manhood are then that speaks to the fact that your father was present in your life as a child and set a precedence for you. You have not had these standards affirmed in anyone you've met previously. Your admission of the inability to be punctual on a consistent basis speaks to a level of discourtesy that you've developed towards your external community. You've learned to live within your own bubble but, overtime this has been lacking. This is also one of the reasons that you've made the clothing investments such as you have, you're still trying to insulate yourself from the world, whether through concealing language or layered fabrics, there's a desire to behold something that holds mystery to those around you. You have learned that your uncommunicativeness has created a peculiar type of intrigue about you but, this only serves for transient relationships. No man in his right mind will enter into matrimony with a mystery. You have to come to grips with why you choose to scheme rather than disclose. I can give you this hint: your level of dashing hopes in people has caused some of this secrecy and also tardiness. You've learned to live with let-downs early on in life so, you make sure every life experience is totally on your terms even down to when the experience will begin chronologically."

Baba Freeman then proceeded to pour a glass of the alkaline water from the glass pitcher that was sitting next to his chair. While he was drinking the libation, Mama Freeman took it upon herself to ask a question of Nile and Kenya. "How did you feel when you were sitting down and writing these thoughts out?"

Kenya began, "I felt naked. I felt really exposed and vulnerable. I didn't think what I had written had so much depth or revealing that much about me but, I did have a feeling that I was uncovering more than I could immediately see. It's easier for me to communicate my thoughts off-line but, I find when I'm standing face to face with someone 90 percent of the time I go into a very yin disposition where I'm just receiving what's being given. A lot of times people get frustrated with me because of this. They assume I'm in agreement with what they're saying to me and when they find out, usually later on, that I held my opinions to myself it causes problems. So, this exercise was good in that it made me look at my sentiments about certain things directly. Now, because Nile read his first, I will say that when I read mine I felt like I didn't complete the task properly. I was told to write a profession to him and I didn't even address him. I spoke very generally and took the opportunity to speak more to the problems I see; rather than what I see being well -standing in the relationship he and I already have."

"Good. Nile?"

"I felt silly, initially. I just felt like every time I attempted to write my feelings down it became cluttered and too wordy. As I was writing I felt insecurity, ineptness, and a little too "soft" for my own comfort. I don't have an issue with thinking abstractly but, to actually share my thoughts in a poetic manner was unusual. I would do it again though because, when I was done I felt a tremendous freeing from it all. There's something about speaking abstractly that makes me feel more complete in my formulation. I felt a presence as I wrote of a mothering energy sitting on my right shoulder and encouraging me to articulate myself however I felt I wanted to. It was liberating, in that sense."

The young couple had been traveling their road towards union for two months but, during that time had unearthed many deep rooted issues that they both carried for years and were oblivious to. The Freeman's were investigating each and every notion they'd held concerning family and introducing new data to them that they'd need in order to make the relationship work. They were being called to answer for every action and idea and to determine its origins and worth. They both discovered that they had used a lot of their time to work in the community and serve those who they felt were less fortunate as a means to avoid dealing with their own intrinsic issues. They had hid their own problems amongst the mountains of responsibilities they'd subconsciously made weighty and pressing. This was a self regenerative mind conjuration that they had to expose in order to deal with it. The Freeman's had them deal with any latent pathologies but, also gave their interactions structure and reason so that within the two months that they'd been courting they'd learned more about one another than they had the entire time they'd known each other. Kenya and Nile learned how and why they attracted one another into their life-time experiences. They each held a key, through specular behavior and character, to one another's perplexities.

Mama Freeman had instituted a communication restriction on the two so that they were only allowed to speak to one another via telephone for five minutes per day. They were still able to organize events together and continue their community work but, on an as needed basis. This was a time that they were to learn other ways of communicating with one another and the value of the precious time that they were able to share. Baba Freeman had told them that it'd be best that they not make a habit out of speaking on the telephone for extended periods of time because, it was an unnatural mode of communicating that should not be used to express anything of real substance as it did not translate all of the energy and emotion of a dialog properly. They were allowed to write each other hand-written letters.

Kenya found the communication regulation to be frustrating at times but, she eventually realized that she had a silent need for reassurance from Nile that she'd not really noticed before.

"Kenya has so many paternal issues that Nile would have been forced to work against all of her prejudices against men stemming from her father before she would have even slightly let him into her heart, genuinely", said Mama Freeman after the couple had completed their weekly three hour session and been seen off.

"Yes, she perceives her father as abandoning she and her mother when her parents divorced and leaving them culturally desolate. What she calls abandonment issues are actually just her ego's way of making it all about her own pain. She doesn't see that he didn't abandon her. He just found that he couldn't live with her mother anymore. She put herself at the center of that ordeal and hasn't recovered since. Her mother made it about her in telling her that her father left them both. We're doing good work though because she's finally facing some of these demons that she's dressed up and convinced herself were spiritual sages coming to grant her unearthly insight about men. She's not seeing relationships from a place of pain as much as she had been when we first begun", said Baba Freeman while preparing to gulp down more of the alkaline water.

"Nile exhibits classic overachiever stress symptoms. His parents set their expectations so high for him that he never learned to enjoy moments in life on the way to his accomplishments. He was always told to do the best that he could and that's all that mattered, as long as he did his best. This 'best' is an unrealistic benchmark that he'll never see because at any given time he's convinced himself that he could do better keeping his intensity level at 100% in every moment without measuring what was really needed for the occasion. He should have been told his best is enjoying himself; giving whatever he's doing full attention. That would have caused him to learn from each activity and endeavor as opposed to making them all his adversaries. He's learning to honor the moment more though. I can see the nature walk meditations have been helping him with that. Nile is beginning to cease viewing everything we give him as a test and he's looking for the fun in each task. His feminine side is beginning to emerge suitably. This will begin to put this undying affection for

Kenya in its right place", Mama Freeman added while sipping on her passion flower tea.

Nile had offered to walk Kenya back to her place as a way to finagle some extra time with her. Mama Freeman had consented to this knowing full well Nile's intentions but, decided the two deserved a treat as they had been working hard and adhering to all prescribed regulations. "Kenya, I know you wanted to laugh when I was reading my poem. Go ahead and get it out now. You know I wrote it with a plume feather and Egyptian ink", Nile said amusingly.

"Nile, I thought it was beautiful. Your poem brought tears to my eyes. I felt honored. I know it was difficult for you but, I think you may have found a hidden talent. You seem to express yourself well enough, unlike me. I sat there and stuttering and pausing my way through my assignment."

"No it wasn't as bad as you think. You did the assignment. That's the achievement. You articulate yourself very well, you always have. This task was very personal though. When it comes to communicating our own personal feelings about things it's always difficult if you're not used to doing it."

"True, True."

After a loud plane had flown overhead Nile asked, "Kenya, do you regret entering into this courtship with me?"

"Absolutely not", Kenya said halting her stride and turning to face the tall man she walked beside. "This has been the noblest process that I've ever been involved in. It makes me feel regal and I know future family is worth this level of self-directed scrutiny. I don't plan on being like my parents. When I join with my mate I plan on maintaining harmony between us for as long as the Creator wills. No, Nile this is the finest work that I could be doing right now. We're handling the business of family. I'm right where I want to be. You?"

"No, I don't regret it at all. I know that our relationship has become a bit more clinical and I know this is for good reason so that we don't get wrapped up in too much emotion and enter into a union blindly. The little paradise that we created before this has been lost, for the moment. I'm patient and with you I'll experience the emotions that I've always dreamed of feeling with a wombmyn. There's not too many wombmyn I could see going through this process with right now. It's very exposing but, I feel safe with you."

Kenya made a mental note that Nile said, "*Not too many wombmyn*". She wondered if he saw her as replaceable and if their relationship or even his attraction for her had been a product of them both being in the right place at the right time? The thought made her feel less than special. She tried to banish the thought when her consciousness informed her that this was a trick of her human thoughts.

I don't need Nile to make me feel special. I don't need anyone to make me feel that way. I am special. I am not the last wombmyn on the planet and I should feel honored that this beautiful man chose me to be his mate. If I was not here, he would not spend the rest of his life as a bachelor and there are plenty of sisters who could use a good man like Nile. Whew... that was close. Mind, you're a trip.

As Kenya reclaimed her own thoughts she was inspired by a notion and thought it a good time to pose a question to Nile. "Brother, what are your views on plural marriage?"

"I've given this a lot of thought before"

"I bet you have"

"Excuse me?"

"I apologize, that was rude. Go ahead Brother, I won't interrupt again".

"Well, I've never had more than one wombmyn at a time but, I think it's a good thing. I've just not seen it done properly as yet but, I think it's selfish for a wombmyn to grab hold of a man as if he is her property but, then ignore the needs of her sisters. There are plenty of children out here that need the steadfast ambient presence of a man...a father. How do you feel about it?"

"I feel similar. Most brothers who I see engaged in the practice seem to have a male-centric arrangement that benefits no one, other than themselves, and the women are just objectified. Although, done right I think it can bring more peace, wisdom, and spiritual evolution to a family. I'm all for big families and when I have my children I'd want them to never have to enter anyone's public school or day care warehouse. OK, I just wanted to get your take on it, we don't have to get into it now, I just wanted to know if you were open to the idea."

"Yes, I'm open to it but, not looking for it. It's a big responsibility and I have to learn how to govern myself in a way that I am comfortable with before I begin introducing other personalities. I would want to spend a minimum of five years in a monogamous relationship prior to even considering anything like that. I need to establish the framework of my home, foremost. I'm in no rush and you are more than enough woman for me."

At this, Kenya giggled. She loved the way Nile looked at her. His piercing stare would look right to her soul when they spoke. One of the things that attracted Kenya to Nile is that when they spoke he always looked her in the eye. He truly respected what she had to say. It had been her observance that most men chose not to look her in the eyes. They would begin to but, quickly begin to look at her body trying to appraise her or determine what she was working with underneath her garments. She was also told that she had hypnotizing eyes. Because of this she learned to look away when men would speak to her as to not seem "fresh" as her mother had once called it. She honestly did not know what men felt when they looked in her eyes but, she did notice she was able to make them more malleable to her wishes when she looked at them a certain way. Not Nile. Nile was like a stone warrior who was not moved by simple parlor tricks. This attracted her to the man all the more as she saw that he was cut from finer cloth than most and saw a greater worth in her than whatever feeling she could conjure up in him. He was planning to build a nation and wanted her to mother it.

CHILD REARING POST MAR-RIAGE

Children are placed on auction blocks (child support), exploit parental division, suffer from cultural/kinship schizophrenia, agonize over torn allegiance, and are developmentally stunted as a result of the dysfunction of hostile cross cultural parenting. When relationships/families are not child-centric or even love centric these maladies are not far off. This can be worsened in the event of divorce or separation as this division, often, moves the checks and balances of co-parenting and dissolves combined family purpose.

Remember, children do not stay children forever. Through the flippant digestion of time, shortsighted adults are tricked into thinking their children crystallize themselves at the moment most palatable to their parents. This is untrue. Life marches forward and your progeny still have needs of nurturing, tutelage, protection, and all of the responsibilities that you signed up for when you decided to co-create them. Demonizing your child's other parent will only serve to drive a wedge between you and your child, even if you don't see its affects immediately. At some point children mature and they go through their own relationship journeys and the demoralizing, and vilifying of either one of their parents by either parent will cause them to detach from the source of that propaganda. Be mindful of what you say to and around your children; particularly the younger ones as they have nothing to do all day but process your words and actions. Do not underestimate their capacity to reason.

We'll focus more on solutions.

SOLUTIONS

We'd be negligent in our adaptive task of unearthing practical solutions to cross-cultural relationship dilemmas if we did not cite the specific scenarios and possible resolutions.

Food:
A common obstacle is the dietary aspirations and regimen to sustain for our children within a split camp scenario. Repeatedly we'll witness one parent who desires to feed a child food that they consider to be of high nutritional content, such as live unprocessed non-meat food, and contrary to that we'll find a parent who feeds that same child based on desires to pacify, appease, socially assimilate, or even undermine or "out do" the other parent. This, expectantly, can be frustrating and even frightening. Of course, the ultimate solution lies in the ability of both parents to intelligently chart out the most researched and suitable "liv-et" for their child.

- Educating the child/children on healthy eating and its long-term benefits can greatly increase the chances that their eating styles will be self-directed towards the highest vibration they can conceptualize. This will also create a reference for that child as to what proper parenting should be.
- If a concern is based around unhealthy eating while a child is away on a parental visit it would be most advisable to send the child/children with prepared meals to deter the temptation of injurious "food" consumption.
- If parental undermining or socio-dysfunctional assimilation is being performed, the best solution is always to educate your child, to the best of your own illumination, as to the reasons certain eating styles will serve them best.
- Continuously inform your child/children that you feed them this way because you love them and the more you love them, the healthier you'll feed them. Any other way of eating will appear as it is... nutricidal genocide.
- Teach your children how to prepare their own healthy meals and use their current life ambitions as their driving motivations (for example: firefighters need strong lungs so mucous causing foods, such as dairy, starches, and acidic foods should be avoided as they hinder breathing. Doctors need good eyes and steady nerves – carrots and herbal mints....).
- Educating either parent on the benefits and detriments of

certain eating habits can make all the difference. If one truly knows that what they are feeding their child is working against that child's natural innate bodily desire to be, and remain, healthy, then a more significant question of devotion and child-care is warranted.

Spirituality:

Another depressing, discouraging, and vexing scenario is one where various spiritual stances are being exposed to children against the will of one or more parents. This, more often than not, is done by grandparents, step-parents, and former co-parents who've "thrown the baby out with the bathwater" after a breakup.

- Make sure you take the time to truly know what your child is spiritually being exposed to and if you hold an objection, voice that to your co-parent and determine if an agreement can be reached first.
- Never try to indoctrinate your child into any singular spiritual or religious approach. In doing this you'll either "cap" their boundless ceiling of awareness or cause them to resent the notion of spirituality all together in the due course of time.
- Create family rituals that are unique to you and your children. I'd suggest Sun Salutations, nightly spiritual cleansing rituals, and Ancestral Fellowship offerings. These can be custom tailored and distinctly ritualized in a hard to refute/reproduced manner.
- Never vilify your co-parent/in-laws because of their religion or spiritual stance. Typically children love both parents and maternal/paternal relatives alike.
- If your child comes back to you after spending time with their other parent, whom they're **fortunate enough to have and know**, provide the nonjudgmental elucidation and clarity about concepts that may be out of alignment with your higher order thinking.
- Trust that your children have access to endless spiritual resources as their cosmic right/rite. You are not their only source of enlightenment.

Again, education and experience will be your greatest tools.

Social:

There are many ways that an individual can be socially indoctrinated and this can be better innerstood by referencing the chapter on culture. In all likelihood there was a split that occurred in a relationship because of an adversarial socio-cultural stand-off. If you are no longer with your co-parent in a harmonious functional relationship, of any sort, do not automatically assume that your socio-cultural innerstanding is being reinforced in your absence. Each parent has a right to parent in a way that they both feel appropriate based on their level of growth.

Always allow your child the respect of space and reason in order to process what each of their parents has to offer. Your children chose father and mother as their passageway and nurturer of incarnate emergence and evolution, respectively. There's always a design being orchestrated in their lives for the fulfillment of their life's design.

Highlight, sincerely, the greatest aspects of your child's other parent/family members. Do not second guess the choice your child made in the spirit realm prior to spiraling down into the physical one.

Often a parent who's seemingly influencing a child more so in one direction is only able to do so because they've provided an experience, when with that child, that's more structured. To balance this enroll your children in activities and experiences that surround them with young people who mirror their own cultural/social designation (rites of passage, dance, music, martial sciences, drumming, scholastic clubs, kwk...). Creating healthy bonding experiences, allowing your children to attach themselves and ideas within the social structure of a supporting collective can all help to remind them of civic/communal expectations, obligations, and demonstrated support/affection. Ultimately a child will lean towards whichever structure provides the most stability and consistency. In lieu of this, it is best, when possible, to establish and represent one structure even after a break-up. The concept of the family need not be decimated. It can live on in idea and response-ability.

Regardless of what you've experienced with your co-parent/in-laws allow your child the right to see and experience their own TRUTH. Using a child as a bargaining chip, go-between, or carrot on a stick will back-fire. Your child did not come to this planet to reinforce your social/cultural understanding. They came with their own individualized life mission that only they are accountable for. Do not become their stumbling block. However, you *can* control and regulate your own home environment and create the surroundings that unquestionably reflects your cultural attitude. Ensure that children can discern a clear delineation between your way of living and your co-parents/in-laws if they are attempting to hinder your child's growth through the perpetuation of ignorance or malice. Creating a distinctive standard will present less confusion for your child as to what is or isn't acceptable in either environment. **BE** what you teach to your children.

If possible, create a calendar schedule when you and your former co-parent/in-laws can participate in certain events and activities jointly (dinner, museums, plays, performances, kwk...). Let the events of higher vibration and substance serve as your principle references.

SETTLING DUST

Tracey and Spencer
Motherly advice

"Baby, have you been sitting out here all this time on this cold porch? Come on inside before you freeze out here".

"I'm fine, Mother; just enjoying this moon tonight. It's so bright."

"Yes, it is a nice full moon. I guess I hadn't noticed. Tracey, I'll get you a blanket at least to cover yourself with and I'll join you".

Tracey's mother returned with a large down comforter and two cups of hot tea. She had a look of concern on her face but, in the night concealment she appeared ghostly. She studied the stillness of her daughter and smelt the faint odor of wine and cigar smoke in the air. She knew that Tracey only engaged in both acts simultaneously when she was conflicted. She hated to see her child in the grips of anything heavy as Tracey had always been a very sober child who rarely even played with other children unless she was appointed to some role of leadership.

"A dollar for your thoughts?"

"I thought it was a penny, Mommy?"

"That was back when people had wooden teeth darling and a penny could buy you a hotel room for a night and a male escort. Inflation is something isn't it?" At this Tracey chuckled and grasped her Mother's hand in hers.

"Mommy, it's Spencer."

"What has that poop-butt boy done to my baby?", Tracey's mother said quizzically.

"I can't blame him. I'm just afraid of what our future is shaping up to be as a married couple. We're headed in different directions mentally and I think we can make it work if we try. I'm not sure if either of us wants to deal with the hassle. Ever since he started hanging out with this guy we went to High School with he's been unreachable. Everything I say is taken out of context and analyzed for cultural incorrectness. I don't know what to do".

"Child, please... Spencer's going through a phase. You have to learn to just stroke his ego and humor his little tantrums. This is just something that men go through while trying to make their mark. It will soon pass."

"I don't know Mommy; he really seems to be bent on changing his entire life and me along with it. Things were fine for us before all of this. We had a system and it worked well for us. I handled the long term stuff and he executed the plans. Now, all of a sudden he's got all of these ideas in his head about what we should eat and what we should be doing in our leisure time, and down to even what movies we should be watching. I can't take it anymore. This is not the man I fell in love with. He's become so illogical and superstitious. I mean he goes to the cemetery every Sunday because he thinks he has the power to talk to dead people now. He's got these shrines set up in his apartment like some sort of witch doctor. The whole thing is just so embarrassing. I feel like somewhere along the way I just lost complete control of my relationship and it morphed into this circus."

"Tracey, you know your father tried to pull that same mess on me. It was a different time and the names change but the actions are the same. I just had to show your father that what I had to offer trumped whatever else he could think about doing. Whatever he's bent on, you can straighten him out. Girl, you got to learn to use your feminine wiles more. It's the power of us women and you, unlike your sisters, have never chosen to use yours. You can't get everything you want, Tracey, by demanding it. Sometimes you have to take a softer, gentler approach. Let that hair down once in a while, put on some nice perfume, that favorite dress he likes. Spencer has always felt way too secure with you. He's taken you for granted all of these years because he never had to work for you. You were always there. I've always told you that was a mistake. You need to learn to make yourself less available to him; emotionally and ...I can't believe I'm saying this...physically. He needs to know that if he insists on disrupting what you've taken years to build that it's going to be a rough ride. Men are really like dogs."

"Mother, that's a bit much".

"No, hear me out child. Men are dogs and we women; we're cats. Dogs are just big and dumb and drool all over the place. They're easily distracted and their emotions are easy to read and play with. Cats are more sly and subtler. You can hardly ever tell what they're thinking and they have a way of making you want to give them affection because they know how to purr just right. Plus, above all, they're self sufficient!"

"You have a point. You really think I've been too giving with Spencer? I mean I always felt I could be because I trusted him and never thought he'd just flip his wig one day like this. I gave myself over to him completely without a second thought. Now, I feel like I'm worthless in his eyes", Tracey said beginning to cry.

"Tracey, look at me", her Mother said holding her chin up to her. "You are never worthless. You're intelligent, beautiful, hard working, you have your own career, your own car, and your own residence, and there is a string of men who'd cut off their pinky toe just to be on a date with you. You hold the cards. He just needs to be reminded of that."

It had been months ago since Tracey had shared her woes with her mother and received her maternal advice. Since then Tracey had made a concerted effort to make sure Spencer knew that he was no longer a primary part of her life but a secondary fixture. It had been difficult for her, initially, but eventually she found herself fitting into the character of this new womand with greater ease and increased conviction. She reasoned away any feelings of guilt or shame concerning her operating with Spencer using manipulative tactics. She realized that she blossomed into the secrets of womanhood late in life and handling herself with Spencer in this manner made her feel more connected to women like her mother who had found their men, married them, and created a home that they were comfortable with. She presumed that all this time she'd been a fool; providing the backbone for Spencer all of these years to have him turn around one day and tell her that all that they achieved together was a waste of time. She decided she was going to learn to look out for her interest, primarily, and guarantee the sanctity of her mind and life. She had a wedding to plan and wanted to devote her energy to that not the philosophical ramblings of Spencer.

Spencer looked over the parking lot through his office window. He stared at a line of mountains in the distance clothed in the green of pine trees. Peering behind him he saw the message light on his office phone blinking. He remained unmoved by the call of duty and focused his attention on the shape of the mountains beyond the parking lot of his job. Recently he'd been offered a position with a local non-profit that specialized in job placement and community organizing in urban communities. He'd been offered a job as the director of the community outreach division. He'd be taking a steep pay cut but, that didn't matter much to him. Lately, he noticed that he was too exhausted after work to go out and spend any of the money he'd earned as a result of his new promotion. His corner office was always kept too cold and now he was expected to be in the service of this multi-national firm 24/7. He had traveled deeper in the belly of the beastly and he didn't like how it felt. He hadn't told Tracey about the new work opportunity because he was sure of how she'd feel about it. He knew she wouldn't even take it seriously but, he kept thinking about his mother and all of the abandoned potential that she had stored memories of. He knew he did not want to live with any regrets and felt that if it came down to it he could always come back to the corporate world but, felt that he owed himself the experience of trying something different. He wanted to take this position because he had aspirations of opening up his own community center one day and figured this would provide him with the experience and contacts he'd need. Even if it was career suicide it would be his decision. It was time for a direction that he chose on his own. He would retake control of his destiny. As Spencer contemplated he realized he'd already made the choice about the job, he just needed to convince Tracey. He told himself maybe she'd just shrug it off. It seemed as of lately she wasn't too interested in him or his goings on, anyway. She was detached and oblivious to him most of the time. She had even started to dress more revealing and spend more time out with her friends. Spencer figured she may have been trying to have an affair before the wedding but, suppressed this thought as it would cause him to feel a pain deep in the center of his stomach whenever he tried to conjure images of what Tracey may be up to. He sensed that she no longer respected him and was just looking for a way out, at this point. Spencer had always loved Tracey for her support and willingness to listen to him and make sense of his ideas. Now, he hardly spoke to her about anything other than the headaches of their jobs. This distance she made helped him to plan his next moves and in some ways he felt he was even indirectly plotting a course out of his relationship with her.

"Absolutely not!"

"Tracey it wasn't a question. Out of respect for you as my future wife I thought you should know", Spencer said trying to maintain his composure.

"Out of respect! Respect? If you had any respect you would have thought about how this affects us both. Spencer, call the organization up right now and let them know you won't be able to accept their job offer. If it's charity work you need to do we can arrange that but, to throw away your future because you want to become some sort of 'Big Brother' is insanity."

"I already accepted the position so, it's too late for that", Spencer said as cool as he could, knowing this was a lie but felt he needed to give the appearance of a definite position and not his usual approach for counsel and advice.

Tracey narrowed her eyes at him and folded her arms saying, "Then tell them you changed your mind".

"I can't do that. I gave my word".

"Oh so now you're lying to me?? What do you think I'm stupid, Spencer? I'm not one of your soul sistahs who's never done anything but peddled incense and sandals on street corners. I won't be made a fool of by you or anyone else."

"Tracey, why is it so hard for you to honor my own decisions? For years you've told me to take the bull by the horns and show some initiative and when I do that you go completely cold on me and berate my every decision".

"Spencer when you knew how to listen to reason we were fine. Now, it's like something in you has broken and you don't know which way is up anymore. I sense Cordell behind this".

"Tehuti."

"Whatever."

"It's not whatever. He has nothing to do with this so, just leave him out of it."

"Yeah right. Now you stand here and have the gall to tell me that you want to go be a street counselor or social worker or whatever and completely change the plans I've made for us; not to mention throw away the years of work that I invested in getting you to where you are today. This is what you call initiative? No, Spencer, this is a crisis. I'm calling your father; maybe he can talk some sense into you".

"Tracey, this is my choice. For almost a year now we've done nothing but argue and fight and it's dis-empowering me. Do you even ask me how I feel at work knowing how every day I spend fueling another person's dream while I boycott my own? Every morning I pull up to that place looking for excuses not to get out my car. I'll sit and listen to the end of a song on the radio or convince myself that I'm so engaged in my morning talk show that I have to listen until it's over. Sometimes I'll just walk around the perimeter of the grounds a few times before going in. As soon as I pull up to the building I immediately get a stomach ache and have to start downing herb capsules just to keep my breakfast down. I sit there all day looking at the clock and counting down to 5:30 and all I can think about is how I'm giving the best years of my life to someone who actually had the initiative and cour-age to go out there and make their vision a reality. Me...I'm just a sheep in there. It's time that I be something more. I want to have a hand in creating a world that my children will inherit that is better than the one I was born into."

"Spencer, you think you're the only one who has dreams? What makes yours so important? You think there aren't days that I question myself and wonder if I've made the right choices in life? We all go through that. I'm trying to keep you strong and you tell me I'm dis-empowering you?", Tracey said with a storm of emotion welling up in her.

"Tracey, listen to me, please. I don't want you to be hurt. I love you. You're my best friend and I don't want that to ever be compromised."

"And neither do I", Tracey said trying to calm the stirring inside of her.

"Maybe it's time for us to re-look at some of our plans and really be honest with one another."

"That's fine", Tracey said remembering the advice from her mother to remain distant and seemingly detached. She knew she needed to find a way to draw Spencer back in. "As long as you know that I'm not going to marry anyone who thinks they can just jump up and make decisions that affects me without my say-so. There are a lot of men who would cut off their pinky finger to be with someone like me. I'm a great catch and I'm not going to just accept anything".

"Sure, Tracey".

Tom and Sheba

Oba Koso

Tom stood outside of the temple, sweating profusely, where he could hear the sounds of wailing and drumming inside. Unsure of what he'd find inside, Tom was determined to see this through. He'd been told by one of the professors in the African studies department about this place some weeks ago. Tom had approached his colleague with questions surrounding African society and religion in an attempt to understand Sheba better. Her words that he overheard some months ago still stung when he thought back. Tom wanted to understand what he'd been missing and also if Sheba was relaying the principles of this "culture", she spoke of so often, objectively. His colleague had invited him to this celebration at his shrine in order for him to meet with a spiritualist and ask some questions about African culture.

As Tom entered the structure he could hardly believe what he saw. There was drumming and singing of chants in a language he'd never heard before. There was a vast shrine at the back of the room with fruits, liquor, cakes, flowers, and decorated pottery all over it. The entire place smelled of cedar and sage incense and strong alcohol. There was a feeling here that Tom could not place his finger on but, it felt familiar. The closest comparison he could draw was the backwoods spiritual church revivals that he would attend as a child with his grandmother but, this was different. This was more potent and less helter-skelter. Tom edged his way to the front of the semi circle that ran the circumference of the temple and stood right where he could observe everything that was going on. He loved the drumming and was even more transfixed by the dancing. To see senior citizens leaping high in the air and hoisting people onto their backs running them around the room was unreal. Tom could feel himself moving to the rhythms and soon clapping along with the drums, tapping his foot and lip-syncing the chants. Before he knew it, a young woman came up to him and pulled him into the middle of the circle with the other men and danced with him around the circle. It seemed that everyone else performed certain steps based on the musical rhythm but, Tom just did what he felt to the approving cheers of everyone present. He was not expecting this but, he sure enjoyed it. Once that music paused Tom made his way back to the semi-circle and observed a few more dances and rhythms. As a new song began once again another woman came up to Tom and held her breast in front of him. She was beautiful. She wore a gold dress and smelled of amber and lavender. Her movements were so sultry and sensual Tom could not help but, be hypnotized by her. She pulled close to Tom and whispered in his ear, "Oba Koso. Mojuba Kabiyese". She then danced away from him and moved slowly around the room. Tom stood perplexed. He looked around for his colleague but, did not see him. As the temple members went into the next phase of the ceremony with all members addressing the huge shrine an older man walked up to him and pulled Tom to the back of the shrine behind a set of velvet curtains and palm fronds. He beckoned Tom to have a seat and sat across from him. Tom remained silent. He had seen enough on this night to know that it would be best to just go with the flow.

"Sango! I see you there Sango! Why do you only hover over him? Let him be you!"

The old man stood up over Tom and said, "Stand, my son. You came here tonight hoping to find the answers that will bring peace into your home. You've been feeling less than a man lately and your meekness has been taken for weakness."

"Yes, how did you know that?"

"That's not important right now. What is important for you to understand is this. All things that we can see are a sign of things that are happening that we can't see. You danced the dance of Sango this evening and were approached by two women. You only danced with one. The other simply intrigued you for a while. This is your life situation. Your first wife introduced you to spirit living by osmosis but, this new mate has blinded you with her love. Your two children suffer because of your domestic impotency. It's time for you to take the reins of your life and home but, you must walk alone to understand who you are first".

"What do you mean walk alone?", Tom said quizzically. He was amazed at the accuracy that this man had in running down his problem and past. Tom became frozen with awe and sat listening like a captivated child at the foot of a griot.

"This new woman now carries your child. Did you know that?"

"No, I didn't. Are you sure? It is mine though, right? Why wouldn't she tell me?"

"Listen, don't wear an old man out with pointless questions. You will have to part ways with this woman or all your children will suffer... They need to see you at your best, not a perpetual follower but, finally a leader. You can re-unite with her later, if you wish, but you have to build a new home of respect and most of all, honesty. Too many secrets have eaten the foundation of your home and now it rots. Love the mother's of your children and treat them fairly but give these boys and new baby girl all of you. They deserve it. You will receive the mate you deserve but, this one has not dealt with you honorably. She desires to maintain her position of dominance by withholding information that does not originate with her and she has yet to comprehend. Do what you will but, this is what the spirits reveal for you".

With that the older gentleman left the little room and headed back into the crowd of attendees. Just then Tom saw his colleague leaning on the wall opposite the consultation room.

"I see you beat me to it and went and introduced yourself to my instructor. How did it go?", Tehuti questioned.

"That was him? I had no idea; he just pulled me to the side and told me a bunch of things I didn't expect to hear. Dude, my head is spinning right now. I need to step outside and get some air."

"Alright man, don't go far we'll be serving food soon. I know you don't want to miss that!"

Tom stood outside of the shrine and felt the coolness of the night air on his sweat soaked skin. He felt cleansed by the happening and reflected on the words told to him by the Elder man Deep down in his soul, Tom knew what the diviner said was true. He had an impending feeling that he and Sheba's relationship was in very dangerous waters. Being a man who'd already lost one family, he suppressed the thought. However, Tom could not deny the fact that whenever he tried to envision growing old with Sheba he couldn't. He'd force himself to imagine he and Sheba sitting in front of a fireplace somewhere in their older ages surrounded by grandchildren; those images never seemed believable. Tom wondered if Sheba actually was carrying his child or if the old man had been "off" tonight. Tom did detect that the man who spoke to him was devout and even his colleague at work had a sort of righteous humility about him while maintaining an approachable humility. He wondered why Sheba had never taken him to any event like this. Was she like these people he'd met on this night or was she just as "green" as he was? Tom heard a voice in the back of his head telling him that Sheba was ashamed of Tom. Tom realized that Sheba hid this side of her life because she felt he wouldn't understand it or he just wasn't important enough to her to share it with. Sorely, he thought back on the conversation he'd heard Sheba having on the phone and realized why the old man told him he'd have to establish a new home with respect. Sheba loved him but, did not respect him. Tom's eyes began to fill with tears as he said to himself, "I'm a good person. I might not know all of this stuff but, I'm a good person. I don't deserve this". Immediately upon stating this Tom felt a passing of latent hostility. A load had been lifted and he felt his eyes seeing for the first time. Tom turned heel and headed back into the temple to find out who this guy Sango was.

Nile and Kenya
Alpha and Omega

"A healthy family is a nation unto itself and it must contain various interdependent nets or cells in order to function properly. Keep in mind that these nets are outer reflections of what each individual member must strive to maintain internally. A wellness component, a security component, an arbitration component, a resource component, and a coordinator are some of the cells a family must have. Each net should have various subdivisions. For example, the wellness net would include health care, spirituality, dance, drumming, meditation, massage, and so on. The resource net would include a family library, archiving and record keeping, financial resources, home and building supplies, and systems of trade. Each home will have to determine what their internal micro-nation must look like in order to serve their needs, as well as the needs of the greater populace. Every family member will take up position in one of the nets/cells. These components should be discussed and outlined during the courting process that we've been discussing. During the process there should be a time where role identification and even conflict resolution are discussed. Conflict resolution would fall under family government or family arbitration net. This is where you have the opportunity to solidify the family philosophy using whatever guiding principles you've chosen for your family unit. I would suggest putting these things in place during the final stages of your courting process. In this, role identification is imperative. Your courtship should also explain why each of these nets is needed in order to maintain a harmonious balance in your home."

"I will now defer to my Empress to see if she has anything to add." Nile turned to Kenya and awaited her response.

"As so masterfully expressed by my Inkosi, yes role identification is one of the most critical pieces because it assists in keeping the domestic peace. I'd also like to add that as wombmyn going through a courtship we have to have faith in the process and recognize that it is just that, a process. There are no guarantees that you will join in matrimony with your courtship partner and you should not enter into a courtship only focused on that. Take each step of the courtship with great care. The nine

125

months that we've completed goes by much quicker than you think and you'll be cramming many activities and bonding experiences within that time. You don't want to distort the balance of the spectrum. What I mean by that is, it's unwise to choose one shade or color of your relationship with your potential mate as the predominant motivation for being with them or continuing in the courtship. You should observe the full spectrum of their behavior and the color blend that you both make collectively. Be honest about what it looks like. I realized when we went through our courtship that I didn't really have faith in men as I thought I had. Our process showed me that I had some deeply rooted childhood trauma that caused me to see men as temporary givers of happiness who'd always plant seeds of long term pain and, women as being the consistent reality that I felt would never betray my heart. In order to really learn brother Nile I had to open myself up enough to really embrace him, spirit and all. If you're not prepared to enter into this process with an open heart, I'd advise against it all together", Kenya said and looked around the center giving those present a chance to catch up on their note taking.

Kenya and Nile had completed their courtship process and as a condition of completion the Freeman's said they had to conduct a relationship panel and discuss their process with others in their community. The panel discussion had been a tremendous success and the participants listened attentively to the chronology of the young couple's courtship experience. Kenya and Nile hadn't realized the turnout would be so great but, as they progressed through the event they realized why. The average person in their small community had no idea of the science of mating. There had been a group acknowledgement that the standards of attraction and partner selection that were used had been based on norms that didn't necessarily speak to their own social needs and they were eager to discover tools and templates that would guide them through the rough waters of relationship engineering.

"If there are no more questions we're going to bring this to a close. I'd like to just state that when possible; find an Elder..., not an older because there is a difference, to help guide you through your series. You want to perform your series in phases and there should be regular checkpoints. Remember that matri-

126

mony is a contract and it does not have to be a lifetime contract. Sister Kenya and I have drawn up a five year agreement with an optional renewal for our union as we felt that worked best for us both and didn't put any pressure on either of us to deal with anything we may find unacceptable."

"This also was done so that every five years we could sit down and determine any new directions we'd need to take. It keeps this alive and in motion. We decided flexibility would be our family mantra. We want to be open enough with one another to honestly discuss what's working for us and what's not. Also every five years we have to reach our promised benchmarks that we've agreed upon jointly. If this doesn't happen we can option to renegotiate the agreement, amend it, or cancel the contract... peaceably", Kenya added.

Nile closed out the discussion and he and Kenya spent close to an hour exchanging words with the attendees. Nile spoke with Tehuti and listened to his feedback on the event. Tehuti had said he was astonished at how deep he and Kenya had dared to go into one another's past. He thought it commendable that they were open enough to share it with the community. Nile had questioned him about a colleague of his that he said he'd try to bring along. "Oh, Tom? He worked out a sweet deal with the university. He applied for a grant to go to Brazil and research the religious and political systems that carried over from the old country with the enslaved Africans who arrived there. Between you and me, he's going there to initiate into the mysteries of Sango. He's been really into it. He broke things off with his Queen so, he wanted to come here and get some information but had to catch an early light out. He said he thought it would be a good forum for her too so, she may actually be somewhere around here. They still keep a healthy relationship for their child and all. But, hey, I'm glad you and Kenya are doing this. You are an inspiration and model for us all."

The two men made their way further into the crowd and branched off. Nile had to get feedback from Ola and Osunsina Freeman. As Tehuti advanced he bumped into a familiar face.

"Peace, Brother Kwesi!"

"Peace, Brother Tehuti! Hujambo?"

"Sijambo. How have you been? It's been a while".

"I'm good man. All is in alignment"

"I'm glad to hear that. The last time we spoke I know you and your lady were going through it".

"Yeah, we had some mountains to climb".

"So, you were able to come to a resolve".

"Well, I feel so. The sister and I decided that it'd be best to move forward as friends for a time until we both can determine what is best for ourselves and futures. She's still my best friend and we have an undying love and respect for one another but, Brother, I won't have my Ancestors disrespected. That's not even up for discussion."

"I'm proud of you Kwesi. You and Tracey have been through a lot but sometimes you have to leave people where they are and continue to make your way up the mountainside. If they chose to get ravaged and attacked by the jungle predators, there's nothing you can do. You weren't born to redeem any other soul but, your own. But, anyway I'm happy for you. How did you hear about this event?", Tehuti asked.

"The sister, Kenya she teaches a class down at one of the community centers that I manage. I let her post some fliers and figured I'd check it out."

Just then Kenya made her graceful strides in the direction of the two men parting the crowd as she moved. She waved to Kwesi and turned around to say something to someone in tow whom Kwesi could not see. Kenya approached the two men and crossed both of her hands across her chest and bowed her head in greeting. The wombmyn next to her did the same. Kwesi looked at her and was captivated with her glow. She was just so earthy and natural looking. It was difficult for any wombmyn to make much of an impression standing next to Kenya but, this wombmyn had a unique special aura that Tom found enchanting.

Kenya then said, "Brother Kwesi, I have someone I would like you to meet. This is Sheba."

TECHNIQUES

Sun Salutation:

1. Face the rising Sun
2. Hold both hands with palms facing outwards at heart level
3. With eyes closed inhale and exhale, deeply, six times. Visualize breathing in the greatness and fortune of the day's opportunities and exhaling trepidation and thoughts of failure.
4. Say the following: "We greet the soul of the Sun with love and honor. We thank you on this day for your obedience and devotion. Today you will show us the beauty of our life. Thank You, Thank You, Thank You".

Moon Ritual:

1. Face the Moon
2. Cross your arms in an "X" formation over your upper torso
3. Look into the face of the moon. Inhale and exhale, deeply, seven times. Visualize inhaling protection and nurturing while exhaling the thoughts and stress of the day
4. Say the following: "We greet the soul of the moon with love and honor. We thank you for watching over us. Tonight we will rest our minds and bodies. Our spirit will make the unknown known. Thank you, Thank you, Thank you."

The Eye of HRU:

This exercise can be done with two or more people. Two people should sit across from one another in comfortable positions. The two will look into one another's eyes for five minutes. This should be done with absolutely no talking or interruptions. After five minutes each individual must give a narrative of what it is they surmised about their activity partner as revealed through their eyes. This is an excellent activity for individuals in "newer" unions.

Family Mission Statement:

A mission statement can assist in upholding the purpose and culture of any union. It's also an excellent tool to use with children who are shared between parents who are no longer engaged in an intimate relationship. Post your mission statement somewhere it can be seen every day prior to exiting your home. *The following represents an example:*

Our family is a shelter and garden of nourishment for us. We are the ones who will tend the fertile garden through ancestral guidance and spiritual insight and will never pass this honor off to anyone else. These are our guiding principles:

- We are a family of divine beings who value one another.
- We carry the sacred mission of our Ancestors.
- We respect one another and value each other's viewpoints.
- We will always strive to solve our challenges internally, first.
- We are a spiritual family and will make time to commune with our Ancestors.
- We are a family of brilliance and genius who strive for harmony and balance.
- We reward and chastise from within, first.
- We define ourselves.
- Our children are our gifts in life, they are not burdens.
- Our children are the essential priority no matter if they are near our far.
- Our parents are the closest beings to the Almighty Supreme Creator. We will treat them as such.
- We will never use one family member against the other.
- We work together as a unit in order to reach our individual and collective goals.
- Education and enlightenment are vital to our growth.
- We will strive to maintain our own internal economy and support our community through barter and resource sharing.
- We will never meander through life but, will always work to fulfill our purpose.
- We are an inventive family and we use our creative energy for productive purposes; never to harm ourselves, family, or community.

<u>**Sample Courting Outline**</u>

<u>Phase 1 Knowledge 3 months</u>

Discovery	Movies:
Interest and Requirement	Determine based
Mutual consent/interest	on Culture
Physical exam	
Income determination (active working plan)	Books:
Shelter determination	Determine based
Character evaluation	on Culture
No Sexual contact	

Goals:

Personal goals are set and the research preparation is done collectively. This is a planning period.

<u>Phase 2 Wisdom 3 months</u>

Discovery	Movies:
Getting to know one another's interest	Determine based
Outings (Museums, Plays, Cultural Activities, KWK.....)	on Culture
Role identification instruction (3-4 sessions)	Books:
Conflict Resolution instruction (3-4 sessions)	Determine based
No Sexual contact	on Culture

Goals:

This is the period where the couple actually implements the personal goals and strategies they researched in phase one.

<u>Phase 3 Innerstanding 3 months</u>

Further implementation and emergence of products of Phases 1 and 2

Emergence and real world testing of the possible familial unit

Outings

Sexual contact (optional)

Matrimonial agreements drawn up, witnessed, and confirmed

Ceremony (optional)

Produce!

CONCLUSION

Some of you are up in arms about GMO foods, gentri-fication, and the cloning of animals. Why are you not equally enraged by these Frankenstein-like families that are patched and grafted by the wayward? A relationship/family thrown togeth-er haphazardly with little to no regard for individual cultural investment is a disaster waiting to happen. The only possible "family" that can result from this type of social butchering is the suicidal one which destroys itself like a worm at the center of a rose; eating it from the inside out. We must abandon this fantasy of cultural euphoric homogeneity which only exists in stale pon-tification of the unenlightened. Cross-cultural relationships must find uniformity internally or they will further decay society as a whole. This is truth. It's time to look at the monster we've created before the monster kills its maker.

To presume that there is no methodology involved when it comes to building a healthy civilization is mindless idiocy. Your civilization will duly reflect the family, which will only re-flect the individual. A family headed by adults who are moving through life like wounded animals creates a society of aggressive distrustful individuals who will try to hurt anything or anyone that comes near them. Bastard children, single parents, emascu-lated men, women depleted of energy and femininity, treach-erous children, cold hearted disloyal kin, fragmented families, and homes full of resentment and hostility are the by-product of unresolved cross-cultural relationships. The carnage is typically dealt with at the surface level but, regardless if you choose to attack its source or not, does not alter the truth of what has been created. We must reclaim our homes with intelligence and the perseverance that comes from the enduring of time. The rewards may be small, at first, but the process of restoring our torn base must begin now. Whether your breakup is a product of religious, social, financial, racial, or sexual non-congruency, the healing techniques are the same across the board. Ignoring this crucial wisdom annihilates your chances of survival and leaves your offspring confused and feeble. Our families can be impenetrable and our legacy prolific but, continuing this madness chokes out the prospect of seeing this innate greatness that we claim to hold. The entire family must stand with uncompromising nobility.

Consider, with reverence, when you co-create you place yourself in the position of The Creator. You become The Creator if only for a split second. By creating a life, you have by default, created family. This means you have created a community, a nation, a universe. The harmony in this new unit will come from mating compliments not culturally torn or adversarial individuals. This initiates discord.

Today family formation has become a crap shoot because many of us remain unaware of the time honored pattern based methods to creating healthy family that have been ignored for the creation of these "Franken-families" that we mix and match like Mr. Potato head toys...hoping for the best. Establishing sound family can be a streamlined, cookie cutter process. Each child can be the star you hoped for at their birth. Each adult member of the family can see the bliss and peace they know that comes from a balanced family. This is the true business of family and it's time to get down to business. The world is an ever changing place and give thought seven generations in advance when you consider joining with anyone or parting from your current mate. What must you do to create the best reality for your offspring to spring from seven generations from now? Theoretically we are thinking 200 years into the future. What must be done today to improve the quality of life for your bloodline 200 years from today? Join wisely!!!

Your Brother in Oneness,

Yuya

ABOUT THE AUTHOR:

HRU has owned and operated a Rite of Passage organization since 2003 and has served as a professional developer for public schools, universities, and social institutions throughout the east coast training school administrators, social workers, and educators on the finer points of curriculum development and responsible cultural inclusion.

HRU currently facilitates workshops centered on community building, Rites of Passage, African-centered curriculum implementation, and youth empowerment. HRU also, currently, serves as a spiritual advisor and natural healer for a cadre of clients and students through the "Sadulu House Spiritual Institute".

He is a cultural educator, empowerment lecturer, and initiated priest who owns and operates a school of metaphysics, community rearing, and family cultivation by the name of the "Sadulu House Spiritual Institute".

CONNECT WITH ME ONLINE:

HRUASSAAN.COM

TWITTER: TWITTER.COM/HRUASSAANANU

FACEBOOK: FACEBOOK.COM/HRU.Y.ASSAAN

ANU PUBLISHING: ANU-BOOKSTORE.COM

SPIRITUAL SCHOOL: SADULUHOUSE.COM

BLOGTALKRADIO.COM/ENLIGHTEN-MENTANDTRANSFORMATION